Nov '90

The Invention of Memory

THE
INVENTION
OF
MEMORY

A New View of the Brain

ISRAEL ROSENFIELD

With a New Foreword by Oliver Sacks, M.D.

Basic Books, Inc., Publishers

NEW YORK

Library of Congress Cataloging-in-Publication Data

Rosenfield, Israel
  The invention of memory.

  Bibliographical notes.
  Includes index.
  1. Memory.   2. Brain—Localization of function.
I. Title.
QP406.R67   1988   612'.82   87-47514
ISBN   0-465-03592-2   (cloth)
ISBN   0-465-03591-4   (paper)

Printed in the United States of America
Designed by Vincent Torre
89 90 91 92 MPC 9 8 7 6 5 4 3 2 1

To Catherine

CONTENTS

Contents

LIST OF
ILLUSTRATIONS

List of Illustrations

ACKNOWLEDGMENTS

The idea for this book grew out of a series of essays I wrote for *The New York Review of Books.* I am deeply indebted to Robert Silvers for the intelligence and tact with which he helped me set my ideas on paper, and for suggesting that I explore work that I might well have overlooked.

Gerald Edelman kindly accorded me seemingly endless hours of time in which he graciously explained his theory to me. I am grateful to him and to Leif Finkel for comments on earlier versions of this work.

My thanks to Michael Studdert-Kennedy who corrected several errors in the manuscript and suggested an important revision of the section on Alvin Liberman's work.

Ellen Hildreth, Eric Grimson, Tomaso Poggio, and their colleagues kindly received me at the Artificial Intelligence Laboratory at MIT, and it was during those meetings that I came to revise my view of David Marr's work. I am thankful, too, to James McClelland for discussing PDP models with me, though I suspect he might disagree with the discussion in this book.

Others who have been helpful include Sydney Brenner, Alfonso Caramazza, John C. Marshall, Elizabeth K. Warrington, and Richard Kaye. I am grateful, too, to Sandra Witleson and Ed Kingston, who were my hosts at McMaster University in Ontario, where I was privileged to present some of these ideas in a series of lectures;

Acknowledgments

as well as to Benjamin Pepitone and the students and faculty of Saint Cloud State University in Minnesota, who organized and hosted an earlier lecture and seminar.

And my deep gratitude to Charles Rosen for his encouragement and many illuminating comments.

Ronald de Sousa always tolerated my late night telephone calls, helping me clarify just what it was I wanted to say.

I am thankful, too, to my editor at Basic Books, Richard Liebmann-Smith, who spent countless hours patiently listening to me and guiding me as the manuscript took shape. And for their editorial assistance I am grateful to Linda Carbone and Phoebe Hoss.

From day to day Catherine Temerson gave me the moral and intellectual support without which this book would not have been written, and to her I have dedicated this work.

New York
October 1987

FOREWORD TO THE PAPERBACK EDITION

OLIVER SACKS, M.D.

Trained as a mathematician, a physician, a philosopher, and a historian of ideas, Israel Rosenfield has a mind of remarkable range. He has the further, enviable gift of being a born writer and has written admirable books on subjects as diverse as genetics and Freud. But his special gift, his most precious one, is his nose for the most important new theories and unifications in biological science and neuroscience. With intellectual antennae among the most prescient today, he senses new theories, new orientations, almost before they are conceived; sees their ramifying and radical implications (often more clearly than their originators); and spreads their excitement to both intellectuals and the public at large.

He has done this through remarkable articles published in the *New York Review of Books:* most notably in his 1984 essay on David Marr, the great theoretical neuroscientist and mathematician, whose work was unknown to intellectuals before Professor Rosenfield wrote of it; and in his 1986 essay on Gerald Edelman, which appeared before Edelman's own books.

With the publication of *The Invention of Memory*, Rosenfield has gone beyond the role of expositor and critic and brought together (as only he could have done) a fascinating variety of clinical, linguistic, and psychoanalytic observations, which he presents in a startling but, once comprehended, beautifully simple new light—a synthesis at once astounding and compelling.

Neurology, as a science, was founded in the nineteenth century. Its grand passions and assumptions were played out first in France—by Flourens and Broca—and then across Europe. On the whole, with some exceptions (Freud, in his book on aphasia, was a notable one), the consensus of opinion inclined to the view of strict localization—seeing the brain as a mosaic of unchanging "centers," each of these a deposit of fixed images and memories. Thus, expressive aphasia, as described by Broca in 1861, was seen as an impairment of a specific "motor" memory, a "memory for the movements necessary for articulating words"; sensory aphasia was seen as a loss of specific auditory word-images or word-memories; and the alexias and agnosias were viewed as losses of specific visual images and memories. *This is still the prevailing view today.* And it is this view Israel Rosenfield subjects to a brilliant critique and reinterpretation in the first part of this book ("Against Localization").

In particular, he takes the famous case Dejerine described in 1892, which appeared to confirm once and for all the notion of fixed memories and localized functions in the brain, and shows that Dejerine's immensely detailed observations can in fact be interpreted in a completely opposite way to that in which Dejerine himself (and all subsequent neurologists) interpreted them.

Dejerine's patient (with a large lesion in his visual cortex) was able to read numbers (but only individually), was unable to read words (though he realized that letters *were* letters), and was unable to perceive color in part of the visual field. These problems, Rosenfield shows, can be given—indeed, demand—a radically different explanation: namely, that the damaged brain in this patient could not carry out certain *procedures* of an essentially creative and comparative sort. Thus, the loss of central color vision that Dejerine's patient experienced is not explicable as damage to a "color center" stocked with "color images" or "color memories" but must be seen as a breakdown of the brain's procedures for *constructing* color by comparison of three black-and-white images (provided by the sensitivity of the cones in our eyes to different wavelengths). There are no "absolute" colors, no colors in nature. What we perceive as color depends on comparison and context, and this is equally the case with numbers or letters—these are only perceivable, only make sense, as part of a context, a whole.

Dejerine's case has been misinterpreted for almost a century. Rosenfield is the first to give it a true interpretation—or, at the very least, an interpretation of a deep and innovative kind, one that suggests an entirely new, non-mechanical view of the brain.

Such a new and nonmechanical view of the brain is suggested by Rosenfield from many other considerations, ranging from the nature of dreams, "Proustian" memories, and language—all of which we are invited to view in radically new ways—to a critique of existing theories of artificial intelligence and machine recognition.

Rosenfield shows that our currently fashionable image of the brain as a computer—the formal equivalent of the doctrine of fixed circuits, fixed programs, fixed memories—cannot *in principle* explain our powers of perceptual recognition (so dramatically disturbed in cases such as Dejerine's or of the agnostic patient I described in *The Man Who Mistook His Wife for a Hat*); cannot *in principle* describe language or thought; cannot *in principle* explain the uniqueness of individuals and their wonderful power to adapt to a constantly changing world.

We must, Rosenfield insists, have radically different explanations and formulations, a science of the individual and his *procedures*, a science of a completely new kind.

Rosenfield is not the only or first person to feel this deep disquietude. Artists have always felt it; many scientists and philosophers, too. I have myself repeatedly called for "a neurology of the self." I came to feel, after writing on the subject ("Reminiscence" in *Hat*), that I had committed a demonstrable error in following Wilder Penfield in his notion of a cerebral store of fixed memories, and was driven to a state of intellectual crisis quite recently by encountering an achromatic patient (in some ways like Dejerine's)—a patient, I was able to show, who lacked *procedures*, not memories.

It is at this point, when the reader has been brought to a state of crisis—a trembling "What now?"—that Rosenfield presents a wonderful new explanation, or model, or formulation. And this is provided, for Rosenfield and for the reader, by Gerald Edelman's theory of "neural Darwinism," perhaps the first wholly biological approach to the problems of memory and perception.

Edelman, who received a Nobel Prize in 1972 for his pioneering studies in immunology which showed how the immune system could "recognize" invaders, has provided a radical new explanation of the brain's, and the organism's, capacity for perceptual categorizations—its capacity, without being programmed and hard-wired like a machine, to create a perceptual (and semantic) "world" for itself out of the billions of chaotic and unlabeled stimuli that descend on it, perhaps to create consciousness and language without a need for the "innate" capacities postulated by Chomsky.

It was only this year that I was finally "converted" to Edelmanism—or at least found in Edelman's theory of neural Darwinism the most plausible explanation for the astonishing visual adaptations and power of visual categorizations that develop in the congenitally deaf. When I came to write of these, I felt compelled to refer to the theory of neural Darwinism:

> Edelman's theory provides a detailed picture of how neuronal "maps" can be formed, which allow an animal to adapt (without instruction) to wholly new perceptual forms and categorizations, new orientations, new approaches to the world. This is precisely the situation in the deaf child: he is flung into a perceptual (and cognitive and linguistic) situation for which there is neither genetic precedent nor teaching to assist him; and yet, given half a chance, he will develop radically new forms of neural organization, neural mappings, which will allow him to master the language-world, and articulate it, in a quite novel way. It is difficult to think of a more dramatic example of somatic selection, or neural Darwinism in action. [*Seeing Voices: A Journey into the World of the Deaf* (Berkeley: University of California Press, 1989).]

T. H. Huxley was sometimes called "Darwin's Bulldog" and Israel Rosenfield, by analogy, may be called "Edelman's Bulldog." He has not only been the first to broadcast Edelman's importance to a wide (and not just narrowly scientific) intellectual circle, but he has illustrated it by a wealth of clinical and humane considerations that reflect his own wide-ranging mind and sympathies as well. A new and tremendously exciting conceptual organization is plotted throughout *The Invention of Memory*, one of absorbing intellectual interest and beauty. It is one that should attract a wide circle of readers, for its implications are not merely neurological or scientific but have equal relevance to art—and to all of us, to the human condition. What we are given is a new view of human individuality and development, the capacity (and necessity) in each of us to create our own histories, our lives.

"Each person . . . is unique," Rosenfield writes in regard to this (Edelman's) new view. "His or her perceptions are to some degree creations, and his or her memories are part of an ongoing process of imagination. A mental life cannot be reduced to molecules."

Edelman's theory, Rosenfield concludes, "gives us an intuitive sense, at the very least, of what the biological basis of mental life might be." The theory "challenges those who claim that science views individual human beings and other animals as reproducible machines, and that science is little concerned with the unique attributes of individuals and the sources of their uniqueness. Humanism never had a better defense."

Florence, Italy
March 1989

The Invention of Memory

Introduction

Imagination and memory are but one thing, which for divers considerations hath divers names.

—THOMAS HOBBES, *Leviathan* (1651)

THIS BOOK is about a myth that has probably dominated thought ever since human beings began to write about themselves: namely, that we can accurately remember people, places, and things because images of them have been imprinted and permanently stored in our brains; and that, though we may not be conscious of them, these images are the basis of recognition and hence of thought and action. Without them, the myth has it, we could not recognize family and friends, words, or our coat in the checkroom; nor recall telephone numbers or titles of books and movies. Surely we recognize people and things because we match what we see and hear and feel with what is stored in our brains, and we recall them by activating the permanent images stored in our brains. These stored images have been "learned": in order to understand the world, we must first be taught what it is.

Of course, there are moments when we don't remember some vital fact, but eventually it usually comes to mind, so we know that it was always there. Nonetheless, many of us do have trouble remembering, and philosophers, psychologists, and, more recently, neuroscientists have generally tried to explain such failings without questioning the fundamental assumption that there are permanent memories stored in our brains.

It is that assumption that this book questions. What is at stake is more than the nature of memory. Because if memories are not the fixed images that tradition and common sense have led us to believe they are, we must revise our whole understanding of the nature of thought and action and of their biological bases in the functioning of the brain. Until recently, most discussions of the brain have taken for granted the notion of permanent memories. Indeed, the most widely held beliefs about brain function are based on this assumption and derive from nineteenth-century thought.

Late in that century, a series of neurological discoveries began to provide a possible explanation of brain function that has become an almost dogmatic tenet of contemporary thinking about memory and, consequently, about mental function in general. Paul Broca's discovery, in 1861, that loss of the ability to speak could be accounted for by a relatively small lesion on the left side of the brain was quickly followed by the discovery of other language centers that appeared to be specialized for different linguistic tasks, and of areas of the brain that controlled movements in specific parts of the body: the hands, the fingers, the tongue, and so on. Other areas were shown to be responsive to sensations in specific parts of the body and limbs. By the end of the nineteenth century, many neurologists had concluded that the brain consists of a collection of highly specialized functional regions which control, for example, speech, movement, and vision. Not only was function localized and specialized, but memory, too, was divided into many specialized subunits. There were memory centers for "visual word images," "auditory word images," and so on. Failure to recall could, therefore, be explained as the loss of a specific memory image (or center) or as the brain's inability to "search" its files due to a break in the connecting nerves. This view of the brain led to a series of brilliant clinical studies at the end of the nineteenth century, in which the exact sites of brain lesions were predicted from patients' symptoms and confirmed at autopsy. The most important theoretical consequence of these studies was the doctrine of localization of function.

Yet a careful examination of these studies—which are often cited in contemporary medical literature as the basis of modern approaches to neurology and brain function—shows not only profound doubts about the approach, even in the work of its most ardent supporters, but telling evidence that throws the entire enterprise into doubt. Modern neurology may be built on incorrect assumptions about how the brain functions. Not only may the doctrine of localization of function be misleading, but the fundamental assumption that memories exist in our brains as fixed traces, carefully filed and stored, may be wrong.

Indeed, without the belief in permanent memories there would have been no doctrine of localization of function, and neurologists, psychologists, and philosophers would have been forced to find an explanation for the apparent specific losses of function associated with brain damage in terms that might have shed greater light on the nature of memory itself. For the inaccuracy of memory has often been observed. Deeply troubled by its unreliability, Sigmund Freud argued against localization of function—without, however, abandoning the notion of a permanent memory. He suggested that memories were fragmentary and that recognition therefore could not be simply a matching of perceived with stored images. He observed that bits and pieces of a person's past are often manifested in dreams and neurotic symptoms, and are only recognized as "memories" when linked to emotions. Crucial to the Freudian view is the idea that emotions structure recollections and perceptions.

The full significance of this discovery may have been missed by contemporary neuroscientists and psychologists. For Freud was in effect describing the functioning of the limbic system (a set of interconnected structures deep inside the brain), long before discoveries in the 1930s suggested its importance in emotional behavior. More recently, limbic structures have been found to affect memory as well. But these recent discoveries were foreshadowed long ago, when Freud noted the fundamental role of emotion in all recollection. His theory may well have provided a more complete understanding of the limbic system and its role in brain function in general than do many of the piecemeal neuroanatomical studies being published today.

Just how much can be learned from Freud is perhaps reflected in the widely misunderstood discoveries of the Canadian neurosurgeon Wilder Penfield beginning in the 1930s. Penfield noticed that electrical stimulation of certain areas of the brain in conscious patients elicited what he considered to be recollections of "forgotten" experiences. Believers in localization of function and permanent memory traces could not have wished for more compelling evidence. It has been shown recently, however, that the "memories" are fragmentary impressions, like pieces of a dream, containing elements that are not part of the patient's past experiences. Furthermore, they occur only when there is activity in the limbic system. In order to have the sensation of a "memory," an emotional link (limbic activity of some kind) appears to be necessary. Indeed, limbic activity may also be important for establishing a coherence, an order, to memories.

But then, are memories veridical? And if not, what might they be instead? And if perception, according to the traditional view, is based on permanent memory traces (an image seen being matched to an image stored in the brain), what is the nature of perception if memories are not permanent? How do I know I am looking at a table if there is no image of a table stored in my head?

Two very different kinds of answers to these questions can be found in contemporary neuroscientific research. One draws its inspiration from the nineteenth-century doctrine of localization of function and from computer simulations, suggesting ways in which visual, tactile, and auditory stimuli are transformed in the brain into more or less accurate representations of the physical world. According to this view, the world is "computed" into perceptions which are then compared to previously learned images stored in the brain (or, in simulated studies, to information encoded in computer memories). There is no perception without prior "learning" (images imprinted in the brain by the environment), though it is unexplained how the images during the initial encounter with information are recognized as worthy of storage.

An opposing view challenges the implications that perception itself necessarily represents a veridical view of the environment and that perception and recognition are independent brain functions. Rather, it is argued, the brain *categorizes* stimuli in accordance with past experience and present needs and desires; and this categorization constitutes the basis of perception and recognition. What we see depends not on any computations but on what we have seen and experienced in the past as well as in the immediate present. In our initial encounters with the environment we will try various ways of categorizing stimuli, and those that lead to meaningful or useful behavior will be reinforced.

Proponents of this view claim that experiences, feelings, and thoughts differ widely from person to person and that these differences cannot be accounted for by any processes as rigid as computations. The world around us is constantly changing, and we must be able to react to it not in terms of previously stored, fixed images that no longer match anything in our surroundings, but in a way that will take account of the new and unexpected, as well as of our individual past experiences. We need not stored images but *procedures* that will help us manipulate and understand the world. If we want to pick up a pail of water, the movements, the muscular coordinations we used yesterday may no longer be appropriate given the different amount of water in the pail, the different clothes we are wearing, and so on.

Procedures are essential to recognition, too. When we see the number *3*, its meaning will be different if we see it alone as *3*, or as the number *36* or *391*. Is there a specific memory image for every possible use of *3*, for every use of the letters of the alphabet—in short, for the enormous changes in significance that symbols (and objects) have in different contexts? We need a theory of the brain that can account for how we can give a sense to stimuli in terms of their present context and our individual experiences. It is not fixed images that we rely on, but recreations—

imaginations—the past remolded in ways appropriate for the present.

The biological basis for such an approach to memory and brain function is described in Gerald Edelman's theory of Neural Darwinism. His work highlights the categorical nature of recognition and its deep relation to motor activity—our past and present explorations of the environment. It suggests that perception and recognition are not independent brain functions, and that the Darwinian principles of selection can help explain the perceptual categorizations that form the basis of memory and recognition. The selected structures, it is argued, are groups of neurons that react more strongly to particular groups of stimuli than to others. But there can be considerable overlap in the way they react to environmental stimuli. For example, a particular dream image may represent more than one person. These neuronal groups are organized into sheets, called *maps*, and the interactions among the numerous maps—and the fact that all the maps are connected to a motor output and to the initial sensory input—categorize information. The past is restructured in terms of the present. Perception and recognition, then, are part of the same unitary process.

In fact, the concepts of memory as procedure and of perceptual categorization were implicit in the doctrine of localization of function. But the localizationists failed to ask themselves why the apparent specialized centers exist. Why would the brain have so many apparent memory centers when what is needed is an ability to fit the pieces together, not take them apart? We don't read letters; we read words and sentences. But in order to make sense of words and sentences we must be able to recognize the many different ways in which identical stimuli can be organized, and this means being prepared for orderings of words we have never encountered.

What look like localizations are different ways of grouping stimuli—parts of a process of creating possible appropriate combinations and orderings of stimuli. The environment doesn't *teach* the organism what it should know; the organism must make its own sense of the environment, and there is no specific way in which this can be done. The "specialized centers" are just part of the larger combinatory tactic (the procedures) of the brain. Their activity makes sense only in terms of the activity of other centers and of the setting in which the organism happens to be. Even some of the computer simulations used in the "computational" approaches to brain function captured the need for procedures that can make sense of stimuli, rather than stimuli that could tell the brain, or the computers, what to do. But rather than be guided by deep biological principles such as Darwinian selection, these researchers paid homage to the superficial observations of localization and apparent permanent memories. The brain is a biological structure. Only in terms of biological principles will we be able to understand it. It is the burden of this book, as outlined in the following paragraph, to establish the importance of these principles.

Part 1 is a critical reexamination of the clinical discoveries that established the doctrine of localization of function. Because of their presuppositions about memory and brain function, the nineteenth-century neurologists overlooked crucial details in their case studies which would have given a broader scope to their work. Important objections were raised by John Hughlings-Jackson and Sigmund Freud in their arguments against localization of function. But even in our own day this part of their work has gone largely ignored, and the contemporary heirs of the localization view, those who believe the brain is a collection of highly specialized functional units that may or may not be anatomically localized, have nearly succeeded in creating a dogma. The deeper objections to localization, however, leave this modern version equally untenable. In part 2 the argument against localization and permanent memory traces is further developed in an examination of recent work on speech perception. The theme of perceptual categorization emerges as crucial to our understanding of the brain. Part 3 shows the nineteenth-century intellectual roots of work in machine intelligence and the consequent failure to recognize what it could tell us about memory. Finally, part 4 discusses the theory of Neural Darwinism, giving us a biological basis for a new understanding of the brain.

I hope that from this study a view of memory and brain function will emerge that will provide reasons for a reexamination of the philosophical and intellectual implications of much current work in the neurosciences. I believe that a view of the biology of mind is beginning to emerge that is far different from what many scientists and philosophers have suggested in the past decade.

1

Against Localization

> What can this memory possibly be, if it is really the result of the fixation in the brain of the impression received by the eye? The slightest movement on the part of the object or the eye and there would be not one image but ten, a hundred, a thousand images, as many and more than on a cinematographic film. . . . In those diseases which correspond to local lesions of the brain, that is in the various forms of aphasia, the psychological lesion consists less in an abolition of the memories than in an inability to recall them. An effort, an emotion, can bring suddenly to consciousness words believed definitely lost. These facts, with many others, unite to prove that in such cases the brain's function is to choose from the past, to diminish it, to simplify it, to utilize it, but not to preserve it.
>
> —HENRI BERGSON, *The Creative Mind* (1911)

Introduction: Localization versus Holism

NINETEENTH-CENTURY neurology was dominated by two opposing schools of thought. Early in the century the Austrian neuroanatomist Franz Gall and his disciples claimed that, to those practiced in the art, an examination of bumps on a person's head revealed talents and psychological characteristics; traits of character, he held, were controlled by specific regions of the brain. Gall had a fashionable success in France, but was ridiculed by the leading neurologist of the day, M. J. P. Flourens, who had performed experiments on birds' brains. At the height of his fame in the 1840s, when he defeated Victor Hugo for membership in the Académie Française, Flourens believed that he had conclusively demonstrated that activities such as walking and flying are not dependent on any particular region of the brain. The brain functions as a whole, he argued, and it is impossible to predict the specific effects of any form of damage.

In 1861 the French neuroanatomist Paul Broca demonstrated that damage to a specific region on the left side of the cerebral cortex causes severe language problems, such as the inability to speak fluently. This was the first serious challenge to Flourens and the "holistic" school. Subsequently, the German neurologist Carl Wernicke found another region on the left side of the brain that apparently controlled different aspects of language, including the ability to understand speech. Wernicke argued that the region on the left side of the brain that had been discovered by Broca was somehow responsible for translating language formulated in the brain into the mechanical movements of the vocal cords, the tongue, and the mouth. A band of fibers called the *arcuate fasiculus* connected Broca's region to the region that Wernicke had discovered; and Wernicke believed that the region he had discovered was responsible for the recognition, or sorting, of speech as distinct from other sounds. Clinicians soon found that such "localization" of brain functions explained many other patterns of neurological disorders in addition to those affecting language.

Localization of function was the principal issue at the Seventh International Medical Congress, which met in London in 1881. At that meeting, Frederick Goltz, a forty-seven-year-old professor of physiology at the University of Strasbourg, opened a suitcase and removed the damaged head of a dog. The dog, he explained, had survived four major operations on its brain before it was killed, and its mental and physical functions had been badly impaired. But not a muscle of its body was paralyzed, not a spot on its hide was robbed of sensation. It was not blind, nor had it lost the sense of smell.

Goltz's purpose in demonstrating this damaged dog was to prove that brain function was not localized. Dogs might become imbeciles if they lost most of their brains, but they could still run, jump, hear, and smell.

David Ferrier, then a thirty-eight-year-old London physician, had performed a series of experiments on monkeys at the West Riding Lunatic Asylum in 1873 and had come to a very different conclusion. At the same meeting, Ferrier showed two monkeys from which he had carefully removed specific parts of the brain. One monkey had a paralysis of the right arm and leg; the other monkey was deaf, but otherwise quite normal. Ferrier concluded that different anatomical areas of the brain are associated with different functions.

A committee of experts then examined the brains of Ferrier's monkeys and Goltz's dog. They supported Ferrier's claim, noting that the brain of Goltz's dog showed considerably less damage than Goltz had stated. Localization of brain function had won the day at the Seventh International Medical Congress.

Much was implied by the victory of this new doctrine.

Against Localization

For it meant that memory and recognition are also localized functions, with visual images, words, and numbers, for example, each stored in separate anatomical regions of the brain. If there was little concern with the nature of memory itself, this was because then (as now—indeed for as long as recorded history) it was generally assumed that we can remember because we have fixed memory images in our brains. The vividness and apparent accuracy of memory gave conviction to this view. Failure to recall, failure to recognize, is an inability to revive a memory image for one reason or another. The inaccuracies of recollection and recognition were evidence of partly damaged or unretrievable images; they were not considered evidence that memory images might not exist. So the new localization doctrine parceled memory into separate anatomical units, each specialized in accordance with the function of that part of the brain. Nobody pretended to understand the mechanisms that created the fixed images. That is a physiological question; its resolution would tell us little or nothing about the *nature* of memory.

These assumptions helped shape the doctrine of localization of function, as much as they helped make sense of a large body of clinical material. The given has always been that, ultimately, memory must rely on fixed images. But it is this assumption that the clinical evidence should have been used either to support or to deny, for as it turns out, the evidence is hardly overwhelming. Many clinical cases were, and are, misinterpreted because the idea of a fixed memory has not been seriously questioned. And the ways in which that evidence suggests a very different view of memory have been largely overlooked. In the nineteenth century, by contrast, there was some uncertainty about the nature of memory. Curiously, one scientist who suggested that not all memories are necessarily fixed, Paul Broca, was the first one to convince the medical world that brain function is localized. What he said about memory has gone unnoticed, though it presents a serious problem for the dogma of localization.

Paul Broca: The Case of Tan and Motor Memory

In 1861, Paul Broca communicated to the Société d'Anthropologie in Paris a brief description of the autopsy findings on a patient who had lost the power of speech and had died the preceding day: "We have every reason to believe that, in the present case, the lesion of the frontal lobe was the cause of the loss of language."[1]

The patient, a fifty-year-old man, had been recently admitted to Broca's surgical ward at the Bicêtre Hospital with gangrene of the lower right leg. He had been subject to epileptic fits since infancy, and had worked as a lastmaker until the age of thirty. At that time he had lost his speech, though it was not certain whether this had happened suddenly or gradually.

That same year, he came to Bicêtre, where initial reports noted that he seemed intelligent and able to understand everything said to him. But to all questions he answered *tan, tan,* and gestured significantly. When not understood, he would become angry and would utter the curse *Sacré nom de Dieu.* Fellow patients called him "Tan" and considered him egotistical, vindictive, and nasty, and those who especially disliked him called him a thief.

His odd behavior was probably a consequence of his brain lesion, though he was never considered insane or in any way unstable enough to require transfer to the lunatic asylum. Indeed, to most people he was "a man who acted perfectly reasonably."[2]

After fourteen years at Bicêtre, Tan gradually became fully paralyzed on the right side of his body and was eventually required to be completely bedridden. He had been some seven years in this state when, following complications, he was transferred to Broca's surgical ward. Broca reported:

The state of his intelligence was difficult to determine accurately. For sure, Tan understood almost everything that one said to him; but since he was only able to express his ideas and desires with movements of his left hand, he had greater difficulty making himself understood than understanding others. He was best when he had to respond with numbers, opening and closing his fingers. Several times I asked him how many days he had been sick. He answered on some occasions five days, and on others, six days. To the question how long had he been at Bicêtre, he opened his hand four times in succession and then put out one finger, making twenty-one years, which was exact. The next day I repeated the same question and I got the same response; but when I wanted to ask him a third time, Tan understood that I was testing him and he became angry and used the same curse I have already mentioned. . . . There is no doubt that this man was very intelligent, that he could think, and that he still had, to some extent, a recollection of things past. He could even understand complicated ideas. Thus I asked him to tell me how his paralysis had begun and progressed. He made a sign with his left index finger meaning "Understood!" Then he showed me successively his tongue, his right arm, and his right leg. It was perfectly natural that he attributed his loss of speech to the paralysis of the tongue.[3]*

*Tan's tongue was *not* paralyzed, though he apparently mistakenly believed that this was the cause of his difficulty.

Tan's inability to speak, Broca claimed, was the consequence of a single lesion, about the size of a hen's egg, on the left side of his brain. And though his linguistic abilities appeared to be grossly impaired, Tan's loss was limited to a single, albeit important, linguistic function. As Broca wrote in 1861:

Those who study such cases for the first time might, because of insufficient analysis, think that the faculty of language has been lost. But it remains complete since the patients have perfect understanding of written and spoken language; and since those who cannot write are intelligent enough (and one has to be in such circumstances) to find a way of communicating their thoughts; and that finally, those who can read and write, and who have free use of their hands, readily put their ideas on paper. Therefore they know the meanings of words, spoken as well as written. Language as they used to speak it remains familiar to them, but they are unable to execute the methodical and coordinated movements that correspond to the required syllable. What they have lost is therefore not the faculty of language, not the memory of words, nor the actions of the nerves and muscles needed for the articulation of sounds, but the ... *faculty of coordinating the movements required by articulated language. . . .*

The nature of this faculty and the place it must be assigned in the hierarchy of cerebral functions might make one hesitate. Is it not, after all, a kind of memory and those who have lost it have lost, not the memory for words, but the *memory of the procedures required for articulating words?* Don't they, as a consequence, find themselves in a state that is comparable to that of a child who already understands the speech of those around him, who knows the difference between blame and praise, who can point to objects others name, who has acquired a host of simple ideas, but who, in order to express them, can only mutter a single syllable? Little by little, after innumerable trials, he succeeds in saying a few new syllables. Nonetheless, he still makes mistakes and says, for example, *papa,* when he wants to say *mama,* because at the moment of pronouncing the latter word he no longer remembers the position in which he must place his tongue and his lips.[4] [Italics added.]

Whatever the nature of the image used for recognition (Broca probably believed it was a matching of words heard with words stored), reproduction of that image in speech is hardly a simple matter. But having learned how to articulate monosyllabic words, the child is confronted by a new set of problems:

Soon he knows well enough the mechanism of a few simple syllables that become easy to pronounce without mistakes or hesitation. But he still hesitates and makes mistakes with more complicated and difficult syllables. When he finally has learned to say several monosyllables, he has to acquire a new experience in order to learn how to go from one syllable to another, and in order to pronounce, instead of repeated monosyllables, that make up his initial vocabulary, words made of two or three different syllables.[5]

Knowing how to say *tell*, *if*, and *phone* will not necessarily allow a child to say *telephone*. Putting single syllables into multisyllabic words requires new procedures, just as putting learned words into sentences requires new procedures. If Broca had gone a bit further in his analysis, he might have hit upon the root of the problem: the precise articulatory gestures used to utter a particular syllable depend, in part, on the syllables that precede and follow it (see part 2). There is no one procedure for saying *telephone*. How we articulate a word depends, in part, on the particular sentence we are saying, the rate at which we are speaking, the emphasis we want to place on the word, and whether we are speaking in a casual or a formal style. What then does it mean to say that there is a memory for procedures? Do we store in memory every possible procedure for every word in our vocabulary? How could we? For we are constantly using words in new ways (and hearing them used in new ways), so that the necessary procedures cannot be stored in our brains. Broca argued that the memory for the procedures for articulating words is different in kind from that for the words themselves, writing in 1861 that "this gradual perfecting of articulated language in children is due to the development of a particular kind of memory which is not a memory for words, but a memory for the movements necessary for articulating words. And this special memory is in no way related to other memories nor to intelligence."[6]

But if the procedures used in uttering a given syllable vary from sentence to sentence, so, too, our recognition of words depends on the sentence in which they are uttered. The idea of fixed memories fails to take into account the importance of context in both recollection (the procedures for uttering a word) *and* recognition. Broca's discussion of a memory for procedures required for articulating words, the "particular kind of memory which is . . . a memory for the movements necessary for articulating words," should have been pursued in the latter half of the nineteenth century, because the fundamental problem of context, which seems so baffling in describing speech, is relevant to *all* forms of memory. Instead, neurologists thought they could solve the problem by positing different memory centers, each containing permanent images that are specifically related to the function of that particular region in the brain. The crucial question was ignored. To those neurologists, localization of function was at issue, and the notion of memory was self-evident. But the nature of memory is far from self-evident, and a careful study of it would have put in doubt the doctrine of the localization of function.

Wernicke and Lichtheim: Specific Memory Centers and Fixed Images

In 1874 the German neurologist Carl Wernicke added precision to the doctrine of localization of function when he showed that auditory word images appear to be located in a memory bank separate from that containing the images of the articulatory movements for words.

It was in this sense—separate anatomical locations—that Broca's two kinds of memory were now elaborated. For in addition to the area discovered by Broca, Wernicke noted a second language center, farther back in the brain, today known as "Wernicke's area." Broca's area, Wernicke claimed, is concerned with producing the coordinated movements of speech, while Wernicke's area contains the "auditory word representations"—the records of individual words. And the two areas are connected, he predicted, by a band of fibers. He went on to explain different clinical syndromes in terms of damage to either one or the other of these speech areas, or to the connecting fibers.

This argument achieved its most elaborate form in an article by the German physician Ludwig Lichtheim, published in German and English in 1885. Lichtheim claimed that the language area of the brain could be represented as a collection of interconnected functional centers:

The schema is founded upon the phenomena of the acquisition of language by imitation, as observed in the child, and upon the reflex arc, which this process presupposes. The child becomes possessed, by this means, of auditory memories of words (auditory word-representations) as well as of motor memories of co-ordinated movements (motor word-representations). *We may call "centre of auditory images" and "centre of motor images," respectively, the parts of the brain where these memories are fixed.* They are designated in the schema by the letters A and M. [See figure 1.1A. Auditory information enters the auditory image center when word sounds are recognized: this is route *a A*. Articulatory movements originate in the "motor center," and are conducted to the speech organs via pathway *M m.*] When intelligence of the imitated sounds is superimposed, a connection is established between the auditory centre *A*, and the part where concepts are elaborated, B. [Italics added.]

Reading and writing were also explained in terms of specific memory centers:

These are acquired in connection with the exercise of speech, and are hence intimately connected with it; the same nervous paths are, to some extent, brought into play. Reading postulates the existence of *visual memories* of *letters* and *groups of letters*. We may learn to understand writing through the connection between such visual representations (centre *O*) [see figure 1.1B] and auditory representations: by spelling aloud we bring the auditory centre into action, and thus establish a connection, through the path *O A*, between *O* and *B*; in reading aloud, the tract *O A M m* is thrown into activity.... [In writing] the necessary movements have to be learnt, and associated with the visual representations; this can be done through the commissure *O E*, designated by *E*, the centre from which the organs of writing are innervated.[7] [Italics added.]

This model of the language centers, Lichtheim reasoned, explained several clinical syndromes. For example, if one's memory center containing the fixed motor

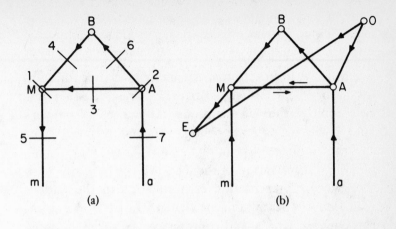

Figure 1.1.

Figure a: Lichtheim's schema of the speech apparatus. *M* stands for the motor speech center (Broca's area). Destruction of this center, indicated by *1*, causes Broca's aphasia. *A* represents the auditory speech center, and its destruction —*2*—causes Wernicke's aphasia. The numbers 3, 4, 5, 6, and 7 represent damage to nerve fibers connecting the different centers, which causes what are known as the conduction aphasias. *B*, what Lichtheim called the concept center, represents not a specific region of the brain as do *M* and *A*, but various regions from which the speech apparatus can be activated. Lichtheim claimed that most of the symptoms found in the different kinds of aphasia could be accounted for in his diagram.

In figure b, Lichtheim suggested how a center for the visual representations of words, *O*, would be connected to a motor center innervating "the organs of writing." (See text for further details.)

SOURCE: Ludwig Lichtheim, "On Aphasia," *Brain* 7 (January 1885): 436, 437.

representations (M) is damaged, voluntary speech will become impossible; one will not be able to repeat words one has heard, to read, or to write spontaneously or to dictation. Yet the patient will still be able to understand spoken and written words, since such understanding depends on the intact memory center for the fixed auditory word representations (A), and to copy written material, since the visual memory center (O) is intact, as is the center E, from which the organs of writing are innervated. This syndrome, Broca's aphasia, is associated with damage to Broca's area.

Similarly, destruction of the memory center for auditory representation (A), Wernicke's area, causes a specific combination of symptoms, known as Wernicke's aphasia. Such a patient no longer understands written or spoken language—speaking, reading, and writing depending on activation of the memory traces in the auditory word-representation center. Nor can the patient read aloud, repeat words, or write to dictation. Yet writing, copying words, and voluntary speech are still possible—each of these activities, according to Lichtheim, depending on centers whose memory traces have not been damaged: that is, writing depends on the idea center activating the writing motor center (B to E); copying, on the visual center activating the writing motor center (O to E); and speaking, on the idea center activating the center of motor images (B to M).

Broca's (motor) and Wernicke's (sensory) aphasias are the two most important examples of language disorders due to brain damage, described by nineteenth-century neurologists. In both forms of aphasia, hearing and vision are perfect. In the motor aphasias the expressive function, the power of speaking, is lost; whereas in the sensory aphasias the expressive functions are perfect, and the patient can speak and write but can neither read nor understand speech. The loss of the motor images of words results in the inability to speak; and the loss of their visual memory images results in the inability to read or write. As Wernicke noted, there is plenty of storage space in the brain: "The cerebral cortex with its 600 millions of cells according to Meynert's estimation, offers a sufficiently great number of storage places in which the innumerable sensory impressions provided by the outer world can be stored one by one without interference. The cerebral cortex is populated with such residues of past stimuli which we propose to call memory images."[8]

Giraudeau: A Case of Word Deafness

The evidence for specific memory loss, however, was not always compelling. In 1865 the French physician Armand Trousseau described a patient who could not repeat words such as *curtains* and *student*, but could say *all* and *nevertheless* and could repeat phrases beginning with *all*. Thus he could say *all the students (tous les élèves)* or *all the curtains (tous les rideaux)*, but not the individual words *student* or *curtain*, suggesting the importance of context in recollection and casting doubt on the idea that specific memory traces had been destroyed.[9]

Indeed a careful scrutiny of the clinical problems attributed to specific memory loss suggests that this conclusion might have been a bit hasty. For example, in 1869 the English neurologist Henry Charlton Bastian first described "word deafness," a disorder attributed to the destruction of the memory traces for word sounds. Patients with word deafness can hear sounds, being able to distinguish a ticking watch from a pin falling on a table, and although they can *hear* spoken words, they cannot recognize them. In 1881 Adolf Kussmaul described word deafness as follows:

The patients may have perfectly correct ideas, but the correct expression for them is wanting; the words, and not the thoughts, are confused. They could even understand the ideas of others, if they could only understand the words. They are in the position of persons suddenly set down in the midst of a population which uses the same sounds but different words, these striking upon their ears as an unintelligible jargon.[10]

In 1882 the French physician C. Giraudeau published the following classic description of word deafness under the title "Note sur un cas de Surdité Psychique" ("Note on a case of psychic deafness"):

Marie Bouquinet, aged 40, a laundress, was admitted into L'Hôpital Saint Antoine, under the care of Professor Hayem, on February 22, 1882. In her antecedent history there was nothing that pointed to syphilis or to intemperate habits. She had never before been the subject of any disease; she, however, had never menstruated, and for three months had suffered a constant headache, affecting both sides of the head, with a nocturnal exacerbation of such a character as to render sleep impossible, the headache at times being so violent as to cause her to cry out from the severity of the pain. She had never had vomiting, loss of consciousness, or any epileptiform attack.

For upwards of a month before admission she was obliged to give up work in consequence of the severity of the pain; at about the same time, it was observed that she no longer understood what was said to her, and that she did not answer when spoken to. This information was obtained from the persons who accompanied her to the hospital, as the patient was unable to supply it herself.

Condition on admission—The patient is very stout, there is no fever, the right pupil is slightly dilated, and there is severe headache. When asked her name, she raises her head, but does not answer. Asked a second time, she answers, "What do you say?" and on the same question being put a third time, she says,

"I don't understand." If she is asked a fourth time, she answers correctly, "Marie Bouquinet."

On being asked, "How long have you been ill?" she evinces the same difficulty of understanding, but replies, after a time, "Three months." If she is asked to give her address, she replies, "Perhaps for three months and a half." Being interrogated as to her occupation, she presents the prescriptions of the physician who treated her in the town, and adds, "A white powder" (sulphate of quinine).

On several occasions we changed our mode of interrogation, but the replies of the patient were always analagous [*sic*] to those mentioned above. After having, with great difficulty, made her understand a question by frequent repetition, she answers; but, whatever subsequent questions are put to her, she follows her first idea, and her subsequent replies have no relation whatever to the questions put to her. Sometimes, however, it is impossible to make her understand our meaning at all, and to every question addressed to her she invariably replies, "What do you say? I don't understand. Cure me."

Her hearing, however, is unaffected; there is no discharge from the ear; she hears the ticking of a watch, and turns her head at any slight noise made near her. Vision is good in both eyes, and there is no word-blindness, for she can easily read the headings of the bed-ticket; and to the question put to her, she replies verbally or in writing, after a little reflection. Tactile sensibility is preserved, as well as the sense of taste and smell; and the motor power is unaffected.

Without entering into further details, suffice it to say that the physical affection rapidly increased, and on the ninth day after her admission the word-deafness was complete, and whenever she was addressed, she invariably said, "I do not understand," and then began to weep. The next day she fell into a state of coma and died.

At the necropsy, a sarcomatous tumor of the size of a walnut was found occupying the posterior part of the first and second temporo-sphenoidal convolutions of the left hemisphere; the rest of the brain being healthy.[11]

In 1890 the English physician Frederic Bateman argued that Marie Bouquinet's problems were the consequence of "the *complete* loss of the auditive images of words." In Bateman's view, this case was

a typical instance of a psychical trouble, characterized by an inability to understand spoken words, although the organ of hearing itself was unaffected. The names of objects and persons uttered in the presence of the patient failed to revive in her mind corresponding auditory images, showing that the part of the apperceptive faculty of speech which is in relation with the sense of hearing, was disordered. It will be observed that, although the auditory impressions of words were not revived, the visual and kinaesthetic memories were unaffected, for the patient could read, speak, and write.[12]

But here theoretical considerations seem to have blinded neurologists. If Marie Bouquinet has difficulty understanding speech, the evidence does not justify Bateman's "*complete* loss of the auditive images of words." When a question is repeated several times, be it her name or the length of her illness, she does answer correctly. She appears to be unable to notice any *pattern* to the questions being asked: "After having, with great difficulty, made her understand a question by frequent repetition, she answers; but, whatever subsequent questions are put to her, she follows her first idea, and her subsequent replies have no relation whatever to the questions put to her."[13] It is curious that when asked her occupation she gives the name of the drug she has been prescribed, as if she were following out the logic of the questioning. A physician who is asking a patient about his or her illness and who, after five minutes of questions about when it started, what the patient felt, and so on, then asked "What do you do?" might well be thought to be asking "What drugs do you take?" Ambiguous questions can be understood only in the context of what has already been asked. And this seems to be Marie Bouquinet's problem. She has great difficulty establishing a context in which she can understand the questions being asked. Repetition of a question is a way of creating a context, a way of forcing the patient to concentrate on the question for its own sake and not in terms of previous questions. That she appears to understand some questions more readily than others is, again, an indication of the importance of context to her understanding of what is being asked. As some questions, such as her name and the length of her illness, are, in the beginning of a medical interview, less dependent on what might have gone on before. (Note that the context is important here, too, since she is being interviewed in the hospital.) It is therefore unlikely that Marie Bouquinet had difficulty understanding speech because she had lost memory images of words; rather, her problem was an inability to establish a context in which the words and sentences she heard could make sense to her.

Indeed, it is this same inability, not the loss of memory images as was, and still is, widely supposed, that explains one of the most famous cases in neurological literature and that therefore gives us powerful reasons to abandon the idea of fixed memories. Because if memories change with context, how can they be fixed? In 1891 and 1892 Jules Dejerine appeared to have brilliantly solved a clinical puzzle that proved once and for all that memories must be fixed and that function is localized. It would be difficult to underestimate the influence of Dejerine's arguments on modern neurology, and hence on some schools of philosophy, and it is to that story that we now turn.

Dejerine: The Man Who Could Not Read What He Had Written

For Jules Dejerine, writing in 1891, localization of function was no longer a debatable issue. Of that he, like many fellow neurologists, was convinced. But the success of the doctrine had led to an overzealous reporting of discoveries of new functional centers in the brain. For some, the doctrine seemed to imply that every human and other animal capacity is determined and controlled by an anatomically discrete area in the brain. One example of such overzealousness was Siegmund Exner's suggestion that there is an independent center for writing. This was challenged by Dejerine in 1891.

In his report to the Société de Biologie in Paris in 1891, Dejerine noted that the inability to write is never found as an isolated symptom, but is usually associated with the inability to read. Writing and reading depend on the same memory images, he wrote, and writing "is only learned under the control of vision; . . . [It] is but the act of copying the optical images of letters and words, and the movements of writing are in every way comparable to those of copying an ordinary linear drawing."[14] He went on to describe a sixty-three-year-old man who had been admitted to Bicêtre Hospital in early 1890 with a slight paralysis of the right side of his body, a condition that gradually improved. A few days later, he woke up and discovered that he could not read or write. By then his paralysis had virtually disappeared. He had a perfectly normal facial expression, understood all questions addressed to him, and was able to mimic the questions and expressions of his interlocutors. But he was unable to read either handwritten or printed matter, or to name individual letters: verbal and literal blindness. Yet he had no difficulty naming objects shown to him. Immediately following his attack of verbal blindness, he occasionally had difficulty speaking, substituting the wrong word for that intended (paraphasia). This condition eventually cleared up, but the patient remained unable to read or write (either spontaneously or to dictation) with the exceptions of being able to read his name, one- or two-digit numbers, and the letters *C* and *G*, which he could also write to dictation. He died on 20 November, and the autopsy revealed a single lesion that explained both the inability to read and the inability to write.

Reading and writing, Dejerine contended, depend on a single memory center containing the visual images of words. That the patient could nonetheless read two-digit numbers was, Dejerine thought, easily explained. In the report to the Société de Biologie, he wrote:

The alexia [inability to read] was complete. Both literal [letters] and verbal [words], the patient unable to recognize any letter or word, except for his name and in this case only its general form . . . and not the individual letters. On the other hand, he could recognize numbers as is frequently observed in verbal blindness. We know that Arabic or Roman numerals, algebraic equations, and so on, as well as one's signature, are equivalent to drawings of objects, and not to letters; we learn to recognize them as conventional signs and not as collections of letters. A patient stricken with verbal blindness will recognize, for example, the figure 8, but will be incapable of reading the word *eight*. [15]

Numbers and one's own signature can be recognized, then, because they are like drawings. But why only one- or two-digit numbers? Are they seen as drawings, as multidigit numbers, or as something else? Length would not be a consideration, since signatures, which can be quite long, are recognized. It may seem a minor point but, as will be seen in the following case in which the same problem occurs, the patient's limited ability to read numbers has a very different explanation. Also unexplained by Dejerine is the patient's ability to read *G* and *C*, which Dejerine ignores when calling his alexia "complete." [16]

In any event, on 27 February 1892, he presented a case that provided powerful support for his argument against a writing center and that, for the first time, made it possible to document the anatomical lesions in a case of pure verbal blindness—a case of a man who could write and speak correctly but could not read. The case is in some ways analogous to the previously discussed study of word deafness reported by Giraudeau, but it has had a far greater influence. Though frequently cited, the study has never appeared in English and is difficult to obtain in the original. In his careful and, at times, moving chronology of his patient's discovery and subsequent realization of the gravity of his condition, Dejerine revealed a wealth of details that he used to justify the localizationist approach. So convincing is his case that contemporary neurologists have used it as a model for the understanding of some neurological disorders. And yet those same details suggest that Dejerine's interpretation may have been flawed. Here then is Dejerine's study of the man who could write, but could not read what he had written.

In November 1887 my friend Dr. Landolt sent me at Bicêtre a patient in whom he had diagnosed verbal blindness [inability to read] with faded and colorless vision on the right side. . . . [The patient, Monsieur Oscar C, is] sixty-eight years old and has always been in excellent health. He has never had any serious diseases and has not been alcoholic or syphilitic. He is a man of well above average intelligence. Having been for a long time in textiles, he has acquired a small fortune that has permitted him to live off his private income. He is married and without children. The couple is very close. His wife, who is younger than her husband by a few years, is also very cultivated. She is a particularly gifted musician and she has instilled her tastes in her husband. He frequently plays music with his wife, reading difficult scores and singing, either alone, or with her. He is equally well informed about literature and reads much. It is obvious in talking with him that he is intelligent and well educated. . . .

Monsieur C has always had excellent vision. During the years that he was in textiles, he was engaged in work that was very tiring for his eyes. He invented textile designs, put them on millimeter-size graph paper, and counted the numbers of threads in a fabric, etc. He had never had any migraines or other cerebral problems before the end of October 1887.

Madame C related that on the 19th of October 1887, her husband suddenly felt several attacks of numbness in his right leg, each lasting but a few minutes. In the following days he had several more attacks. . . . Nonetheless he was able to take long walks. . . . [Then, his right arm and leg became weaker, and one day] he suddenly realized that he could not read a single word, *all the while being able to write and to speak perfectly and being able to recognize as clearly as before objects and persons around him.* Thinking that he had a problem with his eyes, he consulted Dr. Landolt fifteen days later in the hope of getting corrective lenses.[17] [Italics in original.]

Following the visit Dr. Landolt made the following observations, quoted by Dejerine:

Asked to read an eye chart, C is unable to name any letter. However, he claims to see them perfectly. He instinctively sketches the form of the letters with his hand, but he is nevertheless unable to say any of their names. When asked to write on a paper what he sees, he is able, with great difficulty, to recopy the letters, line by line, as if he were making a technical drawing, carefully examining each stroke in order to reassure himself that his drawing is exact. In spite of these efforts, he remains incapable of naming the letters. He compares the *A* to an easel, the *Z* to a serpent, and the *P* to a buckle. His incapacity to express himself frightens him. He thinks that he has "gone mad," since he is well aware that the signs he cannot name are letters. If one shows him numbers he is able to distinguish them, after some hesitation, from the letters. Moreover, he is unable to read the copies of letters that he makes. The letters are, in fact, quite irregular. The *Z* is recopied as a 7 or a 1, the strokes of the letters being poorly indicated or badly placed. . . .

He has no difficulties with his memory and though he is fearful of expressing himself, he speaks fluently and without any mistakes. . . .

If shown any objects, he can name them without any problem. He gives the names of all the parts of instruments pictured in a technical industrial manual. Not once does he manifest any problem with his memory. He immediately names and notices the purpose of all the objects pictured in the manual.

When he is shown the newspaper *Le Matin* which he reads often, he says, "It is *Le Matin*. I recognize the format." But he is unable to read any of the letters in the headlines.

When shown *l'Intransigeant*, a newspaper whose format he doesn't know, Monsieur C says after five minutes of thought, "It is *l'International* or *l'Estafette.*" After a spelling lesson of fifteen minutes he is finally able to read the title, *but in order to recall the letters, he has to draw their form with a gesture of the hand while not looking at the newspaper.* . . .

While reading is impossible, the patient does copy his name correctly. He can write fluently and without any mistakes whatever material is dictated to him. But should he be interrupted in the middle of a phrase that he is writing during dictation, he becomes muddled and cannot start up again. Also, if he makes a mistake he can't find it. While he used to write faster and better, now *his letters are larger, written with a certain hesitation*, for, as he says, *he no longer has the control of his eyes.* In fact, rather than help him, looking while he writes appears to disturb him, so that he prefers to keep his eyes shut and wait. He says *looking while he writes mixes him up. When his illness first began and he tried to write, he wrote the letters one on top of the other. Thus, when he wrote his first name, Oscar, he put the "c" on top of the "s."*

Now he writes from memory whatever he wants, but whether it be his own spontaneous writing or from dictation, he can never reread what he has written. Even isolated letters do not make sense to him. He can only recognize them after a moment's hesitation and then only by tracing the outlines of the letter with his hand. Therefore it is the sense of the muscular movement that gives rise to the letter name. In fact, he can easily recognize letters and give their names with his eyes closed, by moving his hand in the air and following the outlines of the letters.

He is able to do simple addition, since he recognizes, with relative ease, numbers. However, he is very slow. He reads the numbers poorly, since he cannot recognize the value of several numbers at once. When shown the number 112, he says, "It is a 1, a 1, and a 2," and only when he writes the number can he say "one hundred and twelve."[18] [Italics in original.]

Dejerine continues with his own observations:

C spends his days taking long walks with his wife. He has no difficulty walking and every day he does his errands on foot from the Boulevard Montmartre to the Arc de Triomphe and back. He is aware of what is happening around him, stops in front of stores, looks at paintings in gallery windows, etc. Only posters and signs in shops remain meaningless collections of letters for him. He often becomes exas-

perated by this, and though he has been so afflicted for four
years, he has never accepted the idea that he cannot read,
while remaining able to write. After their walks, Monsieur
and Madame C play music together until dinner, or Madame C reads to her husband. . . . biographies of musicians,
novels or newspapers. . . . In the evening they play some
more music and then play cards. He is a very good card
player, calculates very well, prepares his blows well in ad-
vance and wins most of the time.

From time to time he becomes very agitated. He cannot stay
in the same place, walks around a lot, etc. . . . Twice he threat-
ened to strangle his wife and then himself afterwards. One day
he overheard someone saying that the surest way of ending
one's life was to jump off the top of the column on Place
Vendôme. . . . This idea became anchored in his head and he
spoke of it when he became excited. . . . One day, having gone
out alone, he went to Place Vendôme and asked the guard
permission to visit the interior of the column. The guard
refused to let him enter, saying that visits were no longer
permitted ever since two people had committed suicide in the
same week, by jumping off the top of the column.

Following this period of agitation his handwriting became
more irregular. . . .

His sense of orientation remains perfect. . . . [But] in spite
of patient exercises and much effort, he has never relearned
the sense of letters and written words, nor has he ever relearned how to read musical notes.

Yet he could learn new music. Thus he learned to sing
the entire score of *Ascanio* and that of *Sigurd,* both of which
appeared after his attack of verbal blindness. His wife
played the scores for him, sang them with him, and told
him the words. After a little practice he could sing the entire score of *Ascanio* without his wife giving him the slight-
est clue for even a single word. He has a perfect notion of
musical rhythm. . . .

The 5th of January 1892, during a game of cards, C complains
of tingling and numbness in the right leg and arm. . . . The
following day he utters one word in place of another (paraphasia), or utters garbled sounds. . . . He is able to mimic extremely

well, and make his wife understand what he wants through gestures and signs of affirmation or negation. His wife gives him a pencil and notices with dread that he can no longer write. He traces on the paper strokes and lines without any apparent sense, as in the example. [See figure 1.2.]

His intelligence remains intact. He understands all questions that one asks him and remains interested in everything that goes on around him. His mimic was extremely expressive, and his pantomime very arresting. . . .

C had the habit of receiving his niece for lunch every Saturday. In order to tell his wife that he did not want [the niece] to come on Saturday he did the following: . . . He got up, went to the dining room, and set the table for the three of them as usual, his niece, his wife, and himself. His wife understood. "You want to talk about your niece?" Sign of approval. "She must be written to." Lively signs of approval. "Tell her that you are sick." Energetic sign of disapproval. "Write to her to tell her not to come." Lively signs of approval and of satisfaction on the part of the patient. . . . On the morning of the 16th of January 1892, the patient died.[19]

In sum, then, for four years Dejerine's patient had presented the symptoms of pure word blindness. During the final ten days of his life, his inability to read became complicated with symptoms of *agraphia*—inability to write—and a paraphasia that finally degenerated into an inability to express himself in either speech or writing.

In the autopsy, Dejerine found two lesions, one recent and one old. The old lesion had destroyed part of the left occipital lobe, an area important for visual function.* In addition, certain fiber tracts had been destroyed during the early period of the patient's illness. The destruction of part of the left occipital lobe, during the initial period of the patient's illness, explained his blurred vision in the

*Destruction of the occipital lobes causes cortical blindness, that is, blindness due to damage to the brain, not to damage to the retinas or to the optic tracts leading from the retinas to the brain.

Figure 1.2.

Various samples of Oscar's writing, before and after his attack of verbal blindness.

SOURCE: Jules Dejerine, "Contribution à l'étude anatamo-pathologique et clinique des différentes variétés de cécité verbale," *Comptes Rendus Hebdomadaires des Séances et Mémoires de la Société de Biologie*, vol. 4, 9th ser. (Paris: Masson, 1892): 68ff.

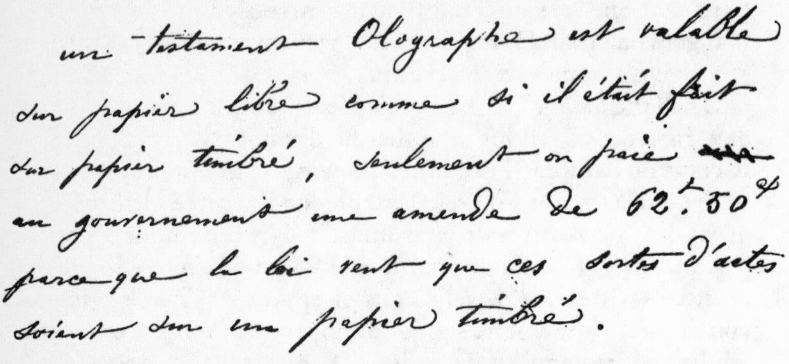

Specimen 1. An example of his spontaneous writing (1886) before the attack. The translation of the text is: *A holographic will on plain paper is as valid as if it were written on stamped paper, except one pays the government a 62.50-franc fine because the law requires that these kinds of deeds be on stamped paper.*

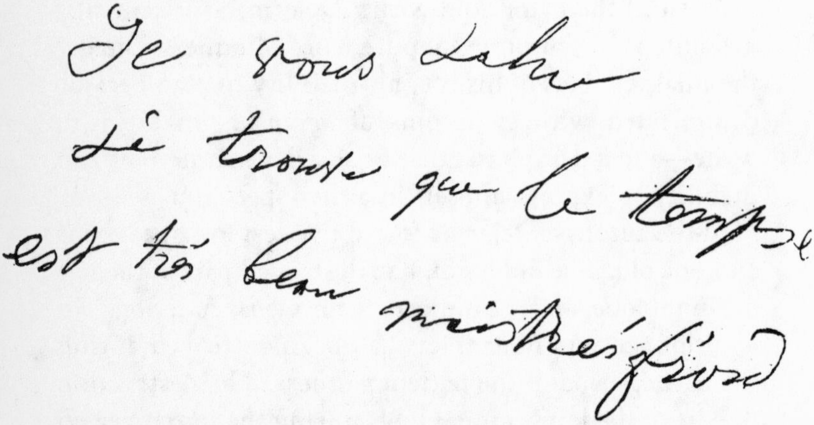

Specimen 2. Spontaneous writing after Oscar's attack of verbal blindness (November 17, 1887). Translation: *I [indecipherable] you I think that it is very beautiful weather but very cold.*

Specimen 3. Spontaneous writing, December 10, 1887. Translation: *I am excessively sick with a cold since yesterday it makes me noticeably* (only partially written out) *congested.*

Specimen 4. Spontaneous writing, January 1888. Translation: *Friday I went to M. Charcot's at Salpetrière who examined me for a long time and showed me to his students saying that I have verbal blindness.*

*Aujourdhui le
17 novembre 1887
je me trouve à
l'hospice de Bicêtre
il fait un temps superbe
mais il fait très froid
quoique le soleil soit
très beau*

Specimen 6. Writing from dictation, November 17, 1887. Translation: *Today the 17th of November 1887 I find myself at the Bicêtre Hospital the weather is superb but it is very cold though the sunshine is beautiful.*

*depuis quelques jours j'ai
commencé à suivre un
traitement par l'électricité
galvanique*

Specimen 7. Writing from dictation, December 10, 1887. Translation: *several days ago I began to follow a treatment using galvanic electricity.*

La ville de Paris où j'habite depuis très longtemps est une fort belle ville

La ville de Paris où j'habite

Specimen 8.

Die Stadt Paris wo ich wohne ist eine grosse und schoene Stadt

Die St, Sta

Specimen 9.

Specimens 8 and 9. Writing by copying from a manuscript (Specimen 8 is in French and Specimen 9 is in German). The French text reads: *The city of Paris where I have been living for a very long time is a very beautiful city.* The German reads: *The city of Paris where I live is a large and beautiful city.*

Specimen 13. Spontaneous writing following a state of severe agitation, December 20, 1890. Translation: *Oscar needs a lot of calm as he no longer wants to be with you that you very much like change that your presence could not relieve him he thinks that it is better that we each stay at home.* (The text was deciphered with the aid of Oscar's wife, to whom he had recounted what he wanted to write.)

Specimen 14. Total inability to write. An attempt at writing during the last days of his life (January 8, 1892). Dejerine wrote about this specimen: "No letter can be recognized in this attempt to write. The patient was aware of the lack of results in his attempts at writing and became impatient, as is evident in the vigorously traced lines that underline the initial attempt at writing."

right visual field. (See figure 1.3.)Dejerine therefore argued that, because of the damage, his patient could not see letters with his left occipital lobe.* The patient did see things on the right—with his left visual lobe—but only poorly. "Because of his right hemianopsia [right-sided blurry vision], this man no longer sees letters with his left hemisphere, and he sees them only with the *right half* of each of his retinas, [which are] in contact with his *intact right hemisphere*." (Italics in original.) Since the language centers are on the left side of the brain (at least in most right-handers), Dejerine posited that the visual information from the intact right hemisphere failed to reach the language centers (containing the "visual im-

---

*Note that Dejerine writes: "*Du fait de son hémianopsie droite, cet homme ne voyait plus les lettres avec son hémisphère gauche, et il ne les voyait qu'avec la moitié droite de chacune de ses retines, en rapport avec son hémisphère droit intact. Il voyait donc ces lettres, en tant que dessins quelconques et les copiait comme telles.*" ("Because of his right hemianopsia, this man no longer saw letters with his left hemisphere. He saw them with the right half of each of his retinas which are connected with his intact right hemisphere. He therefore saw letters as drawings and copied them as such.") This implies that Oscar is *blind* in his left hemisphere, and that letters are therefore only one example of what he cannot see. However, Dejerine adds a footnote here that suggests "obscure" vision in the right visual field due to a lack of color vision, rather than total blindness: "*Je ferai remarquer avec Landolt, que chez ce malade l'hémianopsie droite n'était pas une hémianopsie complètement négative, car il n'avait pas une vision nulle dans la moitié droite de chacun de ses champs visuels, mais bien une sensation de vision obscure. Il était, en réalité, plus hémiachromatopsique qu'hémianopsique proprement dit.*"[20] ("I will point out along with Landolt that this patient's right field hemianopsia was not a completely negative one, for he was not totally without vision in the right side of each of his visual fields, but had a sensation of obscure vision. He was, in reality, more hemiachromatopsic [lacking in color vision in the right halves of each visual field] than literally hemianopsic.")

Some commentators have claimed that Dejerine is suggesting Oscar was totally blind in the right visual field, a suggestion that seems to be denied in the footnote. For example, as noted on page 59, Mayeux and Kandel at Columbia University write, "The patient was blind in the right visual field (indicating damage to the left visual cortex) but otherwise had normal visual acuity."[21]

Others have taken account of the footnote and gone the other way: by *hémianopsie* Dejerine means nothing more than "obscure" vision. But then it is unclear why letters are a definitely excluded element in this blurred view of the world, as Dejerine claims in the opening of the first passage cited. Dejerine's explanation will work, however, with either the "blurred vision" or the "blind vision" interpretation of the text.

ages of words") because of damage to fiber tracts that "we can only suspect without being able to demonstrate either their route, or their existence." On the other hand, no letters were seen by the left hemisphere's visual centers; and, therefore, no information about the letters could be passed on to the language centers. As a result, the letters that the patient did see with his right hemisphere were like "ordinary drawings" and could be copied as such: "But they did not have any meaning for him, for the connections between his two visual centers [right and left] and his visual center for words . . . was inter-

Figure 1.3.

Dejerine's schematic rendition of the connections of the optic nerves and brain centers he believed to be essential for reading, showing the sites of lesions found on autopsy of Oscar's brain, January 17, 1892.

NO: Left optic nerve.

NO': Right optic nerve.

CC: Fibers of the corpus callosum, joining the left and right hemispheres.

Pc: Center for the visual memory for words (angular gyrus).

T1: Center for the auditory memory for words (first temporal convolution—Wernicke's area).

F3: Memory center for the articulation of words (Broca's convolution).

BO: Note partial crossing of optic tracts here so that *dark* area in right visual field is seen by the left side of each retina; fibers from the left sides of each retina connect with other fibers that eventually reach the left occipital lobe (the darkened convolutions at the bottom of the diagram). The left visual field (shaded area) is represented in the right side of each retina, and this information eventually reaches the right occipital lobe (the unshaded convolutions in the lower right half of the diagram). CO, TQ, and GE represent intermediary brain structures. Note the fibers connecting the visual memory center for words (Pc) with the optic lobe and the fibers that pass to the right hemisphere via the corpus callosum (CC), marked 2' and 2". X is the site of the lesion that cut the connections between Pc, the visual memory center for words, and both right and left optic lobes, explaining, according to Dejerine, Oscar's verbal blindness.

Dejerine's diagram also shows fibers, 3, connecting the visual memory center for words to Wernicke's area; and fibers noted as a black line (since they are not visible in this particular slice of the brain) that connects Wernicke's (T1) and Broca's areas (F3). The bifurcating black line represents the connections of the left visual memory center for words with the right hemisphere (5') and left hemisphere (5") motor areas.

SOURCE: Jules Dejerine, "Contribution à l'étude anatamo-pathologique et clinique des différentes variétés de cécité verbale," *Comptes Rendus Hebdomadaires des Séances et Mémoires de la Société de Biologie*, vol. 4, 9th ser. (Paris: Masson, 1892): 86.

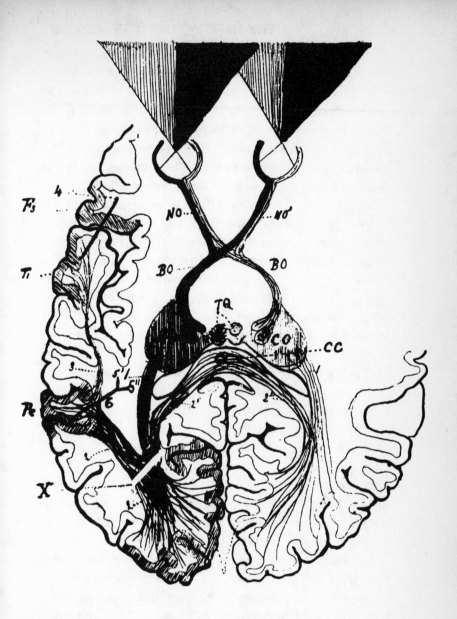

rupted."[22] The visual center for words was not damaged, and thus he could write and even revive the images of the letters by tracing them mechanically with his fingers.

The more recent lesion in Dejerine's patient was "in the visual center of letters (the angular gyrus)." Agraphia is then but one of the consequences of the lesion. Since the visual center is also connected to the "auditory center for words," Dejerine noted, "it is very probable, I say, that the visual image of letters simultaneously arouses the auditory image and the motor image of articulation."[23] Therefore, paraphasia will occur when there is damage to the "visual center for words."

Oscar C, then, had verbal blindness because, according to Dejerine, brain lesions prevented visual information from reaching the language centers containing the memories for visual word images, though the memory center itself was intact and the visual system was at least partly functional. The visual and language centers had become disconnected. In the final days of the patient's life, the memory center (containing the visual word images) was itself destroyed, and the patient developed agraphia and paraphasia, in addition to verbal blindness. This complex of symptoms was now caused by the destruction of the visual word-image memory center and not by the "disconnection" of the visual system from the language area which had produced the initial attack of word blindness.

In sum, Dejerine argued that the inability to read is caused either by (1) the destruction of the "visual images for words"—the images in memory that he claimed are being *copied* when one is writing; or (2) a disconnection between the visual and the language centers, such that visual information never reaches the "word image center" where words can be given a linguistic sense in addition to the purely visual (and nonlinguistic) form derived in the visual centers of the brain.

In the first case—when the visual images for words are destroyed—the clinical symptoms include *both* agraphia (since there are no images to copy) and an inability to read (again, no memory images to which to compare the reading material), as in the 1891 case and Oscar C's final days. This is why *agraphia* is always associated with the inability to read: those very same visual images of words are essential for reading as well. But the reverse is not true: an inability to read is not necessarily associated with agraphia. In the second case there is *only* word blindness—Oscar's original problem. This is caused not by the destruction of memory images but by the inability to retrieve them for comparison with what one is reading; they are "disconnected" from incoming visual information.

The Forgotten Details— Music, Multidigit Numbers, and Color Vision

At the heart of Dejerine's argument is the idea that certain forms of notation, such as numbers and signatures, are equivalent to drawings and are therefore recognizable even when the memory images for language are destroyed or inaccessible following brain damage. Letters and words, on the other hand, can be recognized only when the linguistic memory images are intact and accessible. Modern neurology has paid homage to Dejerine in accepting his approach, though some crucial details have been overlooked in a way that is strikingly similar to Dejerine's own disregard for the same evidence.

In 1891 Dejerine had first made the comparison between numbers and drawings (see pages 31–32), in a case of verbal blindness associated with the inability to write. His patient could read the letters *C* and *G* and one- or two-digit numbers. Unexplained is why he was able to read any letters, and why the reading of numbers, presumably seen as drawings, was limited to one and two digits. In the following year Dejerine described the pure verbal blindness of Oscar C, associated with an inability to read music; again, Dejerine failed to explain why this incapacity was associated with a breakdown of the patient's reading of letters and words. In pure verbal blindness, according to Dejerine, only the visual images of words are lost. Musical notes are certainly not linguistic symbols. Finally, Dejerine's evidence that his patients were seeing drawings rests, in part, on the dubious claim that his patients were copying letters as if they were drawings.

In fact, the reason these patients can read numbers but virtually no letters or words is that single-digit numbers, like one's signature, are always read the same way in every context. A *3* is *three* whether it appears in the phrase "3 apples" or "a 3 percent discount." But the threes in the number *333,333* are each read differently: three hundred thousand, thirty-three thousand, three hundred, and so on. The meaning of a number in a multidigit numeral depends on where it is placed, its context. Recall that Oscar read the number *112* as "a 1, a 1, and a 2." And he could say "one hundred and twelve" only after having repeated the individual digits.

Though he wrote in 1891 that his patient could read one- or two-digit numbers, Dejerine does not give any examples of the two-digit numbers he actually read. Did he read *35* as "three-five" or "thirty-five"? If he could read it as "thirty-five," this suggests that he could, within the very limited context of two digits, note the changes of meaning of a symbol depending on its place. But certainly larger numbers require too many varying contexts for him to have made any sense of what he was seeing.

Words, of course, are like multidigit numbers. Changing a single letter in a word can alter both its pronunciation and its meaning. Its significance depends on what precedes and what follows. This is considerably more complicated than numbers, since the significance of a *3* in a multidigit number depends only on where it is placed, not on whether it is preceded by a 4 or a 3. If one cannot note how the letters (or in a simpler way, numbers) in a word are related to one another, they lose all significance, since there is no sense in which they have an absolute meaning. It is the failure to capture this overall organization—in which identical stimuli, letters, are constantly changing in significance—that is characteristic of patients with verbal blindness. They cannot organize the stimuli in a way that makes sense of the symbols. (See appendix A.)

Reading music, too, depends on establishing complex relations (rhythm, pitch), in this case among groups of notes. The significance of any single note will vary with its musical context. In 1914 Dejerine reported the case of a woman who was an excellent musician and who had lost the ability to read letters and music at the same time.[24] Curiously, she recovered her ability to read written and printed material, but only the treble clef of piano music. The bass clef usually carries the harmonies and is therefore more dependent for "meaning" on the treble clef: more dependent on context. Dejerine's explanation that the treble clef is learned first seems most unlikely. The treble clef usually carries the melody and is therefore less context-dependent. The patient was probably unable to read the bass and treble clefs simultaneously, and therefore no context could be established for the bass clef. (This thesis could be tested by giving such patients music with the melody in the bass clef.)

Therefore, the inabilities to read letters, music, and multidigit numbers have in common not a breakdown of linguistic functions (a loss of the memory images of linguistic symbols) but a failure to organize and reorganize stimuli that use similar signs to signify very different kinds of information. If recognition depends on being able to organize similar stimuli in a variety of different ways, memory, too, must in some sense be based on this organizing capacity. When we recognize a face, we are organizing stimuli in ways that are similar (but not necessarily identical, since the person might have aged) to how we have organized related stimuli in the past. It is the similarity of organization that relates the past and the present. Certainly some images appear to be "fixed"—such as single-digit numbers—but their fixed nature is illusory, since they change their meaning in multidigit numbers, just as letters vary in sense from word to word.

One reason Dejerine argued that word-blind patients see letters as drawings rather than as linguistic symbols is that his patient Oscar could make sense of letters only by comparing them to drawings of objects: "He compared the *A* to an easel, the *Z* to a serpent, and the *P* to a buckle. . . . He thought that he had 'gone mad,' since he was well aware that the signs he could not name were letters."*

But are word-blind patients seeing drawings when they look at letters? Dejerine argues that they must be seeing drawings since they *copy* letters as if they were drawing them. This seems a misleading description: "If he writes easily and fluently, either spontaneously or to dictation, he has the greatest difficulty *copying*. He succeeds only if he keeps the copy constantly in front of his eyes, comparing the letter that he copies, after each stroke, each line, with the original. If he stops, or if one takes the model away, he does not know how to continue the letter, or the phrase he had begun. He copies, in effect, mechanically as if he were copying an ordinary drawing."[25]

When copying letters stroke by stroke, Oscar C was not "drawing" the letters, as Dejerine would have it, but copying them in a peculiar manner. One does not copy a drawing line by line (unless one has not established an overall *Gestalt*) but gets more or less an idea of the whole or the parts one wants to copy, without bothering with the exact details of the original. When we are making a

---

*Some contemporary neurologists have argued that certain forms of aphasia in Japanese speakers can also be understood in terms of Dejerine's distinction between drawings and linguistic symbols. The Japanese use two writing systems: Chinese ideographs *(kanji)* and phonetic characters *(kana)*. The *kana*, or phonetic, system can be used to represent all the words in the language. Because of the large number of homonyms, however, most Japanese writing uses a combination of *kana* and *kanji* to avoid ambiguity. Some Japanese patients with brain damage can read the ideographic form but not the phonetic form. In other cases of brain damage, the opposite is true.

It has been argued that patients who can read the ideographic form but not the phonetic form are seeing drawings (Chinese characters are considered drawings in this view), just as Oscar could see numbers as drawings. The phonetic symbols are linguistic, like letters. But again, contextual changes appear to be the fundamental problem. When Chinese characters or phonetic originals are recognized, it is probable that they have meanings relatively free of context.

copy of any two-dimensional image, we tend to organize that image in certain unarticulated ways. Only if we fail to see any sense of organization in the image that we are copying will we do what Oscar did, slavishly attempt to indicate the length and location of every line in the original. Oscar's limited ability to read numbers and his total inability to read letters and music, then, suggests a visual incapacity to sequence symbolic material, and this explains why numerical symbols can be read with some difficulty and other linguistic and musical symbols not at all.

Finally, Dejerine's patient was unable to see colors in the right side of his visual field, and this defect, too, results from an inability to organize visual stimuli in certain ways. Our understanding of color vision goes back to the nineteenth century when the English physicist Thomas Young proposed that our ability to see a large variety of colors could be explained by postulating three color receptors in each eye. Young proposed that the "color" of each point in a field was determined by the relative responses of the three color receptors, which in turn depended on the amount of light in each wavelength coming to the retina from that particular point. (In fact, there is no "colored" light in nature, but only light of different wavelengths; thus red is associated with long wavelengths of light, blue with short, and so on.) In 1964 Edward MacNichol, Jr., at Johns Hopkins and George Wald at Harvard discovered that there are indeed three types of color receptor pigments in the retina, confirming, in part, Young's proposal. The maximum absorption of the three pigments are in the red, green, and blue wavelengths of the color spectrum.

But the assumption that we see colors because each color receptor directly measures the intensity of light in its particular wavelength, and hence that the individual receptor response determines our seeing a particular color—an argument that would be consistent with a localizationist view—is wrong. Apparently darkness/lightness ratios are determined for each wavelength. For example, if one viewed a multicolored panel through a red filter, the red areas would appear very light, as would the yellow areas. Using a red filter alone, one would not be able to predict which area was red in white light. However, if one then observed the same multicolored panel with a green filter, the red area would become very dark, as it would through a blue filter. "Redness" in white light, then, is the consequence of simultaneous "lightness" seen with the red wavelength receptors in the retina and different degrees of "darkness" seen by the green and blue retinal receptors. Each color has a different pattern of lightness and darkness in the three wavelengths to which the retina is sensitive. And correlating these varying levels of lightness and darkness among the three receptors is essential if colors are to be seen. In part of his visual field, Oscar's brain could not carry out these correlations, again pointing to the same kind of organizational loss—not a specific localized memory loss—that was responsible for his inability to see letters and multidigit numbers.*

*In the 1950s Edwin Land demonstrated how color could be created from black-and-white images. Land prepared two black-and-white photographs of a redhaired woman wearing a green dress. One photograph had been taken with a red filter, the other with a green filter. The photos differed in their black-and-white densities. In one photograph the dress was darker than in the other, the hair lighter, and so on. But they were identical in form and, of course, neither showed any color.

The two photos were then placed in projectors, and the images were superimposed on a screen. A red filter was placed in the projector with the image that had been taken using a red filter. The other projector had only white light. Since the photos were in black and white, and the only color being added to the scene was red, one would have expected a reddish pink image to appear on the screen. What, in fact, appeared was a redhead in a green

Contemporary Misreadings of Dejerine: Geschwind and the Disconnection Syndrome

If the failure to read music and multidigit numbers appears to be a crucial element in Dejerine's study of word blindness, it is remarkable that it has gone either ignored or overlooked in the literature. Richard Mayeux and Eric Kandel of Columbia University's College of Physicians and Surgeons summarize the case as follows:

Dejerine's second patient could speak perfectly well. An intelligent and highly articulate man, he suddenly observed one day that he could not read a single word! He could comprehend spoken language and could write, but he could neither read nor understand written language, including that which he himself had written. The patient was able, however, to derive meaning from words spelled aloud and was able to spell correctly. Even though he could not comprehend written words, he could copy them correctly and could recognize and understand them by manual palpation of the individual letters.

The patient was blind in the right visual field (indicating damage to the left visual cortex) but otherwise had normal visual acuity.[26]

Such oversights and misreadings of the case are hardly surprising, since few have seen the original; its reputation rests largely on Norman Geschwind's revival of it in his influential "Disconnexion Syndromes in Animals and Man," published in 1965. In that paper, Geschwind used Dejerine's study to construct a larger view of brain function as a collection of functionally and anatomically specialized units that are interconnected in higher corti-

---

dress. Land's Retinex Theory attempts to explain color vision along the lines suggested above. What is important here, however, is that color vision is not dependent on specific color memory images, but is a consequence of correlating a variety of visual stimuli.

cal regions. Thus Geschwind claimed, in an argument reminiscent of Wernicke and Lichtheim (see pages 21–25), that in both higher animals and human beings, sensory information—through sight, sound, smell, and touch—is initially processed in the primary sensory areas of the brain. The information is then relayed to neighboring brain regions known as "association areas." In higher animals, but not in human beings, the information then goes from the association areas to the limbic system of the brain—a structure that activates emotional responses such as fight, flight, and sexual approach. For example, the sight of a snake will cause a monkey to flee. If for some reason the connections between the visual areas of the monkey's brain and the limbic system are broken, or disconnected, the monkey will fail to respond when seeing a snake. This disconnection will not, however, prevent the monkey from fleeing should it *touch* the snake—so long, of course, as the touch connections remain intact. For subhuman mammals, each form of sensory information has relatively direct connections to the limbic system, permitting "recognition" and consequent limbic reaction using visual, tactile, or auditory information. There is little mixing of sensory information in animal brains.

In human brains, on the other hand, Geschwind claims (inaccurately—see part 4) that information received through the senses passes from the primary sensory regions to the association areas, as in the higher animals, but circumvents the limbic system. Instead, nerve fibers pass sensory information to a secondary association area (which includes the language centers)—the "association area of association areas"—thus freeing human beings from domination by limbic system responses. Instead of the direct connections between auditory or visual information and limbic responses that are characteristic of animals, human beings have powerful associations between visual and auditory sensations as well as between tactile and auditory, tactile and visual, and so on. All these associations take place in the secondary association areas. Geschwind called them "crossmodal" associations, and wrote: "In sub-human forms the only readily established sensory-sensory associations are those between a non-limbic (i.e., visual, tactile, or auditory) stimulus and a limbic stimulus (fight, flight, or sexual response). It is only in man that associations between two non-limbic stimuli are readily formed."[27]

These associations, Geschwind argued, give human beings the capacity for speech: "The ability to acquire speech has as a prerequisite the ability to form crossmodal associations."[28] In his 1965 monograph, he claimed that language is a consequence of the association of two or more kinds of sensory information, for example, the association of the spoken word *dog* with the visual image of a dog. A disconnection between the visual cortex and the limbic system in the monkey explains why it fails to respond to the sight of a snake (though it certainly sees the snake); the disconnection between the visual cortex and the language centers in Dejerine's patient destroyed his ability to read: though he could see the written words, he could not read them with his eyes. But he could still "read" by using his sense of touch, which was not disconnected from the language centers.

Geschwind's study of disconnection syndromes suggested that psychological capacities, such as recognition of objects, are composites of independent brain operations. A man can see an object without recognizing it, and yet he can touch the same object and have no difficulty naming it.

Dejerine and Bernstein: Movement and Memory

In fact, the power of the tactile sense alone had been demonstrated in 1892 by Jean-Baptiste Charcot, the son of French neurologist Jean-Martin Charcot, when he built an apparatus that permitted one to read by tracing the outlines of letters with one's finger (see figure 1.4). The apparatus consisted of a long wooden stick attached at its upper end to a fulcrum. The lower part of the stick was

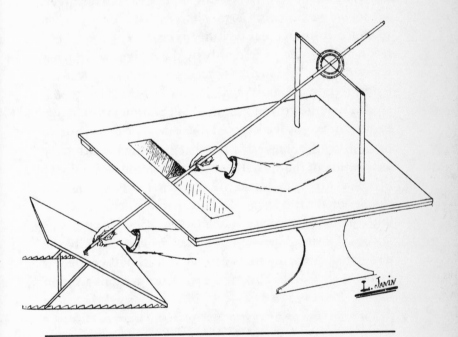

Figure 1.4.

Charcot's apparatus for creating motor images of letters and words in patients with verbal blindness. Note that the lower hand is that of the physician guiding the fulcrum over the letters, and the upper hand is that of the patient. (See text for details.)

SOURCE: Jean-Baptiste Charcot, "Sur un appareil destiné à évoquer les images motrices graphiques chez les sujets atteints de cécité verbale," *Comptes Rendus Hebdomadaires des Séances et Mémoires de la Société de Biologie*, vol. 4, 9th ser. (Paris: Masson, 1892): 237.

guided over the letters by the physician as the patient grasped its midsection. Handwritten and printed material would be somewhat enlarged, so that the movements followed by the patient's hand were often smaller than those used in writing. In a series of experiments on a variety of normal subjects, Charcot noted: "Written letters are more easily distinguished than printed letters; lower-case letters are better distinguished than upper-case letters; model letters are relatively easy, particularly for children; one's own writing is very easy to decipher, others' more difficult. Certain letters that are most often modified in individual writing styles, *F, P, Q, R, S,* can frequently be deciphered only by the individual who has written them."[29] Having used his apparatus to test the identification of individual letters only, Charcot concluded that the greater ease in identification of one's own handwriting—as well as the failure in some cases to identify *F*s, *P*s, *Q*s, and so forth that had been written by others—proved the existence of a graphic-motor center.*

It was this very claim, the existence of a specialized center for writing, that Dejerine had challenged in 1892 when he had successfully explained Oscar's symptoms without positing a writing center. More generally, he had noted, human beings can write with either the left or the right hand. The muscular coordinations used in

---

*In defense of his claim for a graphic-motor center, Charcot recounted how a patient with verbal blindness and paraphasia particularly for names, unable to recall his name, "one day, on my recommendation, tried to write my name, succeeded without difficulty, and hardly having finished writing, cried out, 'Charcot.' This name, that he had himself written, he could not reread a few seconds later. Ever since, when looking for words he uses this little trick."[30]

The example is interesting for reasons quite unrelated to Charcot's argument, for it shows that motor activity (writing) can organize stimuli, making recollection possible. The patient could recall and could recognize what he was writing *while he was performing that act;* but he could not recognize the same written material visually, the movement of his eyes being insufficient, in his case, for organizing the stimuli.

writing the letter *e*, for example, with the left hand are not the same as those used in writing an *e* with the right hand. It is therefore unlikely that the movements of both hands are controlled by a single center, to say nothing of the other parts of the body one might use to write. As Dejerine wrote:

If habit has it, in effect, that we write out of preference with our right hand, that is to say with the motor center of our left hemisphere, we could nonetheless succeed in writing . . . with our left hand, even with our foot. We could even succeed in writing by holding a pencil between our teeth and using the movements of our head to print.

It is not therefore necessary to posit, for writing, the existence of a so-called special graphic center, and even less to locate it in the foot of the second left frontal convolution, since if this center existed, we would at least have to spread it throughout the motor zone of each limb, not only in the left hemisphere, but in the right as well.[31]*

But though he argued that the movements for writing may arise in various brain centers, those movements are still "copies" of visual images of words; therefore Dejerine maintained a belief in fixed memory images. Here, however, he fails to follow out the logic of his own argument. How the visual memory images are copied when one writes remains unexplained. Indeed, the copies are always different. As the Soviet neuropsychologist Nikolai Aleksandrovich Bernstein wrote in 1945:

*And in 1914 he noted: "Whenever the 'interior language' is affected by disease, agraphia appears. In my research I have found writing difficulties in Broca aphasics (motor aphasia). . . . The vocal apparatus is specialized for speech; writing is only one of the ways in which we manipulate our hands. We can only speak with the [vocal apparatus]; we can write with the elbow, the foot, by skating, in a word with any part of the body, provided that it is sufficiently mobile. And there is no difference among these diverse forms of writing. If writing with the hand is easier, it is a question of education."[32]

This is illustrated with great clarity by the example of drawing, perhaps because this type of movement leaves a record which may be conveniently studied. It is easy for everyone to draw a five-pointed star, but we can say with certainty that this picture is made by using only topological and not metric relationships. As proof of this I suggest the experiment of drawing ten such stars in succession and comparing the pictures. I doubt if it is at all possible to make a metrically perfect copy of a similar object without the help of a compass and a ruler, that is, the human motor system cannot attain any high degree of metric proficiency, but it can be said that our motor system is very sensitive to topological distinctions.[33]

Bernstein argued that the localizationist view "would answer perfectly to reality if every central impulse unconditionally governed a single determinate movement, that is, if there existed a one-to-one correspondence between impulses and movements." However, he continued,

this type of one-to-one correspondence does not exist and the cerebral motor area organizes response by deftly adjusting and balancing between resultant external forces and the manifestations of inertia, constantly reacting to proprioceptive signals and simultaneously integrating impulses from separate central subsystems, so that ten successive repetitions of the same movement demand ten successive impulses all different from each other; and the presence in the cortex of localizational equipment . . . begins to seem a very dubious interpretation. I would like to recall here the failure in 1923 of the invention of "a symphony of whistles." An attempt to convert steam whistles into a musical instrument with an organ keyboard failed because any given whistle could not be relied upon to sound the same on every occasion, and its pitch would vary with the pressure of steam, with the number of whistles sounded simultaneously, with the degree to which the steam-channel was clear, and so on, so that it was impossible to obtain a one-to-one correspondence between the keyboard, on one hand, and the frequencies of the tones obtained, on the other.

And furthermore, he argued:

Let us suppose that the cells of the gyrus centralis are in reality the effector centre for the muscles. Let us further suppose that the activity of these cells must be (as is inevitable in the given hypothesis) sharply different from instant to instant on the multiple repetition of a given movement, in relation to changes in the external force field and proprioceptive signals. If we suppose for clarity that we may represent each excited effector cell in the cortex as lighting up like an electric bulb at the moment when its impulse is transmitted to the periphery, then under such an arrangement the effecting of every movement will be visible to us on the surface of the cortex as a zig-zag discharge. The absence of one-to-one correspondence . . . will be obvious in this case because on every repetition of a given movement the zig-zag discharge will be visibly different. Now suppose that this repetitive movement is an automatized act, the realization of a habit of movement, in other words, a conditioned motor reflex. From the discussion above it follows as an inescapable deduction that the conditioned reflex of movement operates each time through a new zig-zag—through new cells; in other words, we arrive at the conclusion that the hypothesis of cellular localization of muscles necessarily leads to a denial of cellular localization of conditioned reflexes. One of the two chess pieces must here be taken, and it is here a very pertinent question which of the two the old-fashioned localizationist would rather sacrifice.[34]

Dejerine failed to see that the procedures of writing themselves create the "images" we set on paper, and that, because they organize perceptual material, procedures are also responsible for recognition. After all, Oscar could recognize words when his hand was guided over printed or written material. The guided motions of Charcot's machine, like those of Oscar being aided in the tracing of writing, organize the tactile perceptions. Oscar's inability to create organized perceptual units for music, numbers, and letters prevented his recognition of these symbols quite independently of any specific memory loss, or even any access to memory images.

Memories, then, are the procedures that are responsible for the organization of perceptions. They are themselves *generalizations* of previous experiences, ways of organizing sensory stimuli that permit them to be related to past experience. When Dejerine stressed that *writing* could be carried out in a number of different ways and therefore is not localized, he, too, was suggesting that memory is procedure, but without seeing this fact as true of all motor acts, including speech. (We can say the same sentence quickly or slowly, casually or formally, with or without a pipe clenched between the teeth: in each case, the precise gestures and the resulting acoustic patterns will be different. Yet the sentence will be the same.*) In spite of himself, he had hit upon one of the crucial failings of the localizationist view and its contemporary heir, modularity, which retains the idea of specialized functional units in the brain without necessarily claiming anatomical localization. Both views derive in part from clinical examples of specific losses, such as the cases already discussed. However, the many ways in which similar motor acts can be performed (with the right hand, the left hand, the foot, and so on), as well as the overriding importance of context in recognition, suggest that neither localization nor modularity adequately explains the nature of brain function. The loss of specific functions is an illusory consequence of brain damage that, as will be discussed in part 4, can be explained in terms of larger functional principles.

*These examples were suggested to me by Michael Studdert-Kennedy.

Against Localization I:
Shattering the Foundation

There are deeper reasons to question the doctrines of localization and modularity. Recognition, according to these views, is possible only when what is seen, touched, or heard is matched with a memory trace stored in a specialized area of the brain; this leaves unexplained the formation of the original memory trace. How does the brain "know" that a particular sound is an example of a word and that a "copy" of that sound is to be stored in the "word-sound-image center"? There are no memory traces for comparison when the word is first encountered. *Therefore there must be ways in which the brain can create classifications of stimuli independently of any specific memory trace; and the procedures used in classification would then be important for subsequent recognition as well.*

Furthermore, a hidden and unquestioned assumption of the localizationist view is that there is specific information in the environment that can become the fixed memory images. But if recognition depends on context, it is the *brain* that must organize *stimuli* into coherent pieces of information. That process depends on the variable ways in which a given stimulus can be interpreted in one context as opposed to another. The brain's ability to categorize stimuli then must depend on something other than fixed memory traces.

Indeed, the localizations, or, in the contemporary view, functional specializations, suggested by the study of clinical material must be illusory, for what is implied is not that the brain creates our perceptions out of ambiguous stimuli but that it *sorts* neatly packaged information coming from the environment. But if there are specific centers that process (or sort) information, as is claimed, each center must decide what is relevant for the next higher center in the structure. If it already "knows" what is relevant, then it has already solved the problem. If the "visual center" knows what kinds of images are letters, words, or decorations, why is a word (letter) memory center necessary? That "memory" must already be in the visual center. How else could it have been sorted out?

On the other hand, if the visual center can *abstract* "words," among its many ways of abstracting a visual scene, but does not know which abstractions are words—or even when an abstraction is in one context a set of decorations and in another a set of letters—other "centers" will be necessary to relate these abstractions to the context and thereby allow the brain to see words and/or decorations. Making sense of the environment would then require a constant interaction among these various (abstracting) centers, and a constant reference back to the environmental source of the stimuli. Clinically, specialized centers may become manifest. But the apparent specializations reflect the limits of the brain's ability to form categories out of stimuli following brain damage. Certain kinds of correlations can no longer be made.

Brain damage causes a rearrangement in the way stimuli will be interrelated. It may prevent some kinds of relations among stimuli from being established and therefore force the brain to substitute others that, in the circumstances, may be the best it can do, but that are hardly satisfactory. It is not memories *per se* that have been lost, but some ways of interrelating stimuli. And therefore the crucial issues are what ways of correlating stimuli are no longer possible, and how those correlations that remain are related to particular environmental settings.

For, though surroundings may be drastically altered, brain activity at one time may be similar to activity in very different circumstances on previous occasions. Therefore sudden changes in one's environmental setting can be very disorienting. One psychological consequence may be depression.

In his 1914 essay "Mourning and Melancholia," Freud suggested that there are many similarities between the grief we feel when a loved one dies and cases of melancholic depression. The parallel is interesting, because it suggests that loss (of someone) may be central to the psychology of depression. This may not sound very surprising, but what is of importance is how one reacts to loss. A curious clue comes from patterns found in the animal world. Konrad Lorenz noticed a long time ago that among ducks and geese the death of one member of a pair leads to a search (with abnormal manifestations) for the missing partner that can last for days. Some of the symptoms of depression may derive from search procedures—attempts to establish new connections between brain activity and a changed environment. Depression during the time of loss (of a job, of a friend, of prestige, and so on) may be a period when the brain is "searching" for a solution to problems that cannot be solved, at least in a relatively brief period of time.

New connections are being sought. Eventually, we may find a way of accepting a substitute for the person we have lost, but this may require a considerable reevaluation of what we desire in our personal relations with others. The solution of such problems may require a reorganization of our patterns of thought and even, perhaps, of our values. The period of rearrangement—

which may involve trial and error—is one in which we may have the hopeless feeling associated with depression. We are recategorizing, reorganizing, our way of viewing the world; and the relations between brain activity and the environment are changing.

In sum, the localizationist and modular arguments rest on the illusion that specific pieces of information can be sorted out by the various specialized centers of the brain. In fact, however, the brain does not sort information; if it did, context would be irrelevant to perception. The importance of context in recognition shows that the nature of information useful to the brain is not predetermined. The brain must determine what combinations of stimuli are useful, and to do this it must create the categories, organizations, and orderings of stimuli that are the information we perceive in the environment. And the creation of these categories requires the cooperation of many "centers," each creating subcategories from which our perceptions are abstracted.

Against Localization II:
Hughlings-Jackson and Cursing

One of the most profound mistakes in the doctrine of localization of function has been the failure to recognize that brain activity is meaningful only in a particular environmental setting. The dissenting views of the English neurologist John Hughlings-Jackson and those of Sigmund Freud have come close to grasping this point.

Against Localization

As Hughlings-Jackson wrote in 1879, "any one will readily admit that the pain of a pin-prick is in himself, not in the pin; and every educated man admits that redness is in himself when he uses the ordinary language, 'This brick is red.' " Stimuli are not imprinted on the brain, Hughlings-Jackson argues, but result in an activity in the brain that comes to be associated with the external object:

> When we say we see a brick, all we mean is that we project into the environment, ideal or actual, the image which that brick has roused in us. This image arisen in us is the survival of the fittest image at the termination of a struggle which the presented brick has roused in us, is the end of the subjective stage; the further stage, or the second stage, is objective—it is referring the image already roused in us to the environment, actual or ideal. The brick is for us nothing more than what it has itself roused in us.[35]

Therefore, contrary to the localizationist view, internal activity is not specific to any object. An internal state has meaning only in relation to a particular environmental setting; similar brain activities can have very different meanings.

It is the ability to create novel or new meanings—by rearranging stimuli in new settings—that is so characteristic of language in particular and of brain function in general. And it is this very ability, as well as its clinical significance, that Hughlings-Jackson captured in his description of what he called "higher degrees of utterance" by one speechless patient:

> A man, for several months under my care in the London Hospital, was absolutely speechless. He never *uttered*, much less spoke, anything but "pooh," "pooh," so far as I or the students or the nurses knew. But I was told by his friends of

three utterances. Once, when he had had enough bread-and-butter, he said "No more." . . . [And] I was told that one day the patient said, with difficulty of articulation, "How is Alice [his daughter] getting on?" A third utterance was, I think, as high, if not still higher, in speech. His son wanted to know where his father's tools were. In reply to his son's questions, the patient said, "Master's." Although here is but one word, where in health there would have been a sentence, there is a proposition; it told his son where the tools were as fully as the most elaborately worded and grammatically complete sentence would have done. It was far higher than the most elaborate oaths, and higher even than such utterances as "no more," "good-bye," "very well," etc. Once more I would urge that speciality in speech ("high speech") is not simply an affair of number of words, nor simply of complexity of their arrangement. We have to consider precise adaptation to special and new circumstances: "Master's" did not come out upon a common and simple occasion, like "good-bye"; it was definitely uttered to signify a very special relation, moreover a new relation. Granting, for the sake of argument, what, however, I do not know, that the man had in health replied scores of times to the same question by that word, or by a fuller proposition containing it, it was specially used for a new occasion, under, that is, very new circumstances.[36]

Brain-damaged patients are often reduced to uttering a few words that are applicable in the most general circumstances, because they are unable to organize a more specific verbal response. Hence they often retain the use of *yes* and *no*: " 'yes' and 'no' give assent or dissent to anything whatever; they are the blank forms of, or stand for, all negative and positive propositions. . . . From their almost universal applicability they are very frequently used; they are the most general, most automatic, and most organised of all propositions." These patients have not lost other words; they have lost the capacity to organize them. "A fire occurred in the street opposite one of my wards in the London Hospital," Hughlings-Jackson recounts, and "a speechless patient of mine cried out 'fire!' Is it not a grotesque supposition that this woman retained only the word 'fire!' "[37] The woman was able to utter the word *fire!* during the emotional excitement caused by standing in front of a burning building—in that context the word organized what she felt and saw. But two days later she was no doubt incapable of calmly talking about the "fire" that had destroyed the building; brain damage deprived her of the capacity to organize her thoughts in a new context.

Emotions, in fact, are powerful organizers of thoughts and actions. Broca's patient Tan could not speak, but he could curse. This is not uncommon and, as Hughlings-Jackson reports, uninformed observers are often misled by these patients' outbursts:

In general the laity cannot be expected to know that swearing, etc., may persist when speech proper is impossible, and certainly not that a higher kind of utterance may persist when the patient is fatally ill. No doubt many apoplectic persons found in the streets are locked up for drunkenness because the policeman does not know that swearing is a very automatic process, which can persist under conditions produced by fatal brain lesions as well as by drink.[38]

Or take the case of Madame B, recorded by the French physician Armand Trousseau: "On receiving a call from a visitor, she rose to receive him with a benevolent smile on her countenance and, pointing to a chair, said *'Pig, Brute, Stupid Fool.'* 'Mrs. B begs you to be seated,' said a relative who was present, and who thus became the interpreter of the patient's wishes thus strangely expressed. Let us note that the acts of this lady seemed sensible, and strange to say, which is not usual in aphasics, she seemed to be neither impatient with nor aware of the foul language she was using."[39] In the circumstances the best Madame B could do was to say *"Pig, Brute, Stupid Fool,"* and though her listeners found this an inappropriate response, Madame B seemed to have found it more than adequate.*

Hughlings-Jackson attributes such emotional utterances to the survival of a lower, more primitive response in brain-damaged patients. Borrowing from the ideas of a French neurologist, Jules Baillarger (1865), he suggests that "spontaneous" responses remain while "voluntary" responses are destroyed.† But the distinction fails to cap-

---

*The translation is in Frederic Bateman's 1890 *On Aphasia*. The original passage in Trousseau reads as follows:

Madame B . . . , belle-mère d'un médecin très recommandable, sans avoir jamais éprouvé d'accidents paralytiques, arriva assez rapidement à des troubles d'intelligence fort singuliers. Un visiteur entre chez elle; elle se lève pour le recevoir avec un air de bienveillance et lui montrant un fauteuil: "Cochon, animal, fichue bête (Madame vous invite à vous asseoir, dit le gendre, qui interprète la volonté de la malade, si étrangement exprimée)." Notons en effet que les actes de cette dame paraissaient d'ailleurs assez sensés, et chose bizarre, qui n'est pas ordinaire chez les aphasiques, elle ne semblait pas s'impatienter ni comprendre le sens des injures qu'elle proférait.[40]

†In 1880 Hughlings-Jackson published the following, rather odd note on the first page of the second part of his series of articles "On Affections of Speech from Disease of the Brain":

I should like to remark that one very general conclusion to which the several facts so far stated, and facts afterwards to be stated, point, was in principle long ago formulated by M. Baillarger. So far back as 1866, 'Med. Times and Gazette,' June 23, I made the following quotations from his writings, which I now reproduce:—

"L'analyse des phénomènes conduit à reconnaître, dans certains cas de ce genre, que l'incitation verbale involontaire persiste, mais que l'incitation volontaire est abolie. Quant à la perversion de la faculté du langage caractérisée par la prononciation de mots incohérents, la lésion consiste encore dans la substitution de la parole automatique à l'incitation verbale volontaire." ("The analysis of these phenomena makes us recognize that in certain cases of this type, involuntary language persists while voluntary language is abolished. As far as the perversion of the linguistic ability characterized by the utterance of coherent words, the lesion is again a consequence of the substitution of automatic speech for voluntary speech.")

I ought to have reproduced this quotation in the first installment of this article, as evidently I am following pretty closely the principle this distin-

ture the relative contextual independence of cursing as opposed to most utterances, which acquire different meanings in each new context. After all, we curse just for the sake of cursing and nothing much is meant by it. But who would say "cortical" or "adumbrate" merely to add emphasis to a remark, or to give the impression of following a speaker's discourse? How these words might be used in a sentence is not necessarily immediately self-evident. To the brain-damaged patient, it is not at all obvious how to use *most* words, because these people have difficulty in establishing the interrelations between the words and the inevitable variations in meaning that occur with each new sentence. It is not that memories have been lost, but that the ability to establish correlations has been destroyed. Those utterances that require little or no such ability remain, giving the illusion that a few specific memories have been spared destruction while all other words have been lost.

Utterances are creations that are deemed appropriate at the moment; and memories or recollections are also creations that appear to be the most appropriate organizations of things seen, heard, and felt at any given moment. Of course, what came before and what may be experienced after are crucial in determining what is and is not appropriate, an ability that Marie Bouquinet lacked, just as Oscar could not note how a letter related to a preceding or a following one. Hughlings-Jackson's studies hint not only at the importance of this organizational ability in the creation of recollections but at the importance of emotions, though he mistakenly assumed

---

guished Frenchman has laid down. For the satisfaction of curious persons, I may say that I give it now spontaneously, no one having drawn my attention to the omission. I fear M. Baillarger's acute remarks have attracted little attention, and I say with regret that I had forgotten them. I do not remember from what book I took the quotation."[41]

that "emotional recollections" are primitive in character. Cursing is not primitive; it is merely relatively context-free.

Against Localization III:
Freud—The Fragmentary Memory

The distinction between *spontaneous* and *voluntary* speech—the assumption that emotional utterances are primitive—does not account for the importance of emotions to recollection. An ability to organize verbal utterances is not sufficient for creating a "recollection" of an event. The sense of an utterance—its significance in terms of previous statements—can vary greatly depending on how emphases are placed; and associated affects or emotions can greatly alter the importance and the significance of a recollection. If there is no emotional link to a recollection, a simple verbal statement of the episode will often go unrecognized, or ignored, by the speaker. Recollections without affect are not recollections. Emotions are essential to the creation of a memory because they organize it, establishing its relative importance in a sequence of events much as a sense of time and order is essential for a memory to be considered a memory, and not a thought or a vision at some particular instant, unrelated to past events.

Sigmund Freud emphasized this very point when he noted that individuals do not recall a past experience that has been separated from its original emotional setting. The experience, he wrote, "remains as though isolated and is not reproduced in the ordinary processes of thought. The effect of this isolation is the same as the effect of repression with amnesia."[42] In emotionally charged circumstances, as Hughlings-Jackson noted, some "speechless" patients suddenly curse, or give forth a "forgotten" word or phrase. Deprived of affect, Freud argued, recollections become unrecognizable: "What remains in consciousness is nothing but its ideational content, which is perfectly colourless and is judged to be unimportant."[43]

So, for example, in the course of an analysis a patient may produce a series of similar, but not identical, statements that appear to be recollections but to which he or she pays no attention. In successful analyses, these statements become "memories" when they suddenly acquire an emotional coloring and the series of recollections are "recognized" as different versions of the same primal scene. Yet these scenes, Freud admits, "are not productions of real occurrences. . . . [They are] products of the imagination, which find their instigation in mature life."[44] Analytic recollections are generalizations, or recategorizations, of past events which derive their significance from the associated emotions; events that become emotionally charged are thereby categorized and "understood." Indeed, for Freud, analytic recollections are significant in the specific context, in the emotionally charged atmosphere, of the transference relationship with the analyst.

If we fail to recognize, or appear to forget, "ideas" deprived of emotional content, the "memory" nonetheless, Freud claims, still exists, unnoticed and unrecognized in part because of the detached emotions, in part because it has become a fragmented and distorted image not unlike the fragmented and distorted images that are the essence of dreams. Thus the "real" meanings of these fragments can be disguised:

Above all there is a striking tendency to *condensation,* an inclination to form fresh unities out of elements which in our waking thought we should certainly have kept separate. As a consequence of this, a single element of the manifest dream [the actual content of the dream] often stands for a whole number of latent dream-thoughts as though it were a combined allusion to all of them; and in general the compass of the manifest dream is extraordinarily small compared with the wealth of material from which it has sprung. Another peculiarity of the dream-work, not entirely independent of the former one, is the ease with which psychical intensities (cathexes) are *displaced* from one element to another, so that it often happens that an element which was of little importance in the dream-thoughts appears as the clearest and accordingly most important feature of the manifest dream, and, *vice versa,* that essential elements of the dream-thoughts are represented in the manifest dream only by slight allusion. Moreover, as a rule, the existence of quite insignificant points in common between two elements is enough to allow the dream-work to replace one by the other in all further operations. It will be easily imagined how greatly these mechanisms of condensation and displacement can increase the difficulty of interpreting a dream and of revealing the relations between the manifest dream and the latent dream-thoughts.[45]

Yet the fragments are all that remain of our "memories" in a state of sleep, "condensations" of many images that refer to many different things, acquiring specific meanings in a context, just as letters acquire significance in the context of words. During sleep we are, as Freud himself often noted, paralyzed and out of contact with our surroundings. Without a context, without an environmental setting, our "memories" are the incoherent fragments Freud describes so well, fragments that may not have any "meaning" or interpretation. Freud's belief in fixed memories compelled him to explain this fragmentation in terms of condensation and displacement, but the fragments are ambiguous at best. In this belief, condensation and displacement could account for the apparent distortions and failures of recollection that are so much a part of everyday psychology. But a memory becomes a memory only in the context of the present; it is organized and given a sense in that context. What we recall we recall here and now. Freud acutely noted the fragments—the ambiguous images—of memory; but their lack of sense is a lack of context, not disguise and displacement.

Memories manifest themselves in the immediate, and therefore differ greatly from the occasion on which they arose. Freud assumes that the dynamic aspects of memory require processes that operate on fixed memory traces. Yet those traces become evident only in dreams and neurotic symptoms, and the character of this material, its superficial confusions and even apparent incoherence, though perhaps "interpretable," is itself evidence not of fixed traces but, on the contrary, of a confused collection of impressions that must be *organized* into a coherent form that we can associate with memory. Curiously, Freud's recognition that dreams must be interpreted to give them a sense suggests that "memories" are also "interpretations" of previous impressions in terms of present circumstances.

Dreams, then, are incoherent because there are no constraints on the organization of these fragments. They "are exempt from mutual contradiction" and there is "no negation, no doubt, no degrees of certainty."[46] Freud failed to recognize that the fragments are nonspecific and become meaningful only when organized, and that the apparent condensations and displacements are evidence of the nonspecificity of the contents and not of the mixing of specific memories. The mechanism of condensation is an illusion created by interpretation in which one seeks a context that can give the image meaning and coherence. But the apparent "correctness" of an interpretation is merely a creation of the moment. It carries conviction in the same way as any recollection or recognition: as an appropriate (or the apparently most appropriate) organization in the circumstances. After all, there are no environmental demands on dreams. When we consciously "remember," the environmental setting, the circumstances in which we find ourselves, becomes a powerful constraint on how and what we can recall, much as interpretation gives meaning to dreams. And although the fragments acquire reference in a conscious state, their ambiguity gives the illusion that they are *condensations* of many images, an ambiguity that the establishing of context through dream interpretation appears to resolve. It was these fragments that Wilder Penfield observed beginning in the 1930s, when he elicited "memories" by direct stimulation of the brain, as will be discussed in part 4.

There are no specific recollections in our brains; there are only the means for reorganizing past impressions, for giving the incoherent, dreamlike world of memory a concrete reality. Memories are not fixed but are constantly evolving generalizations—recreations—of the past, which give us a sense of continuity, a sense of being, with a past, a present, and a future. They are not discrete units that are linked up over time but a dynamically evolving system.

It is therefore odd that Freud felt compelled to argue in 1915 that the assumption of an unconscious is *necessary* because the data of consciousness have a very large number of gaps in them; both in healthy and in sick people psychical acts often occur which can be explained only by presupposing other acts, of which, nevertheless, consciousness affords no evidence. These not only include parapraxes and dreams in healthy people, and everything described as a psychical symptom or an obsession in the sick; our most personal daily experience acquaints us with ideas that come into our head we do not know from where, and with intellectual conclusions arrived at we do not know how. All these conscious acts remain disconnected and unintelligible if we insist on claiming that every mental act that occurs in us must also necessarily be experienced by us through consciousness; on the other hand, they fall into a demonstrable connection if we interpolate between them the unconscious acts which we have inferred.[47]

But continuity is in terms of the present, in our capacity to generalize and to categorize when confronted with the new and unexpected. Much as calling two similar-looking flowers *tulips* establishes a relation between them, a category and hence a continuity, our categorization of present events in terms of past experience (which inevitably we all do) establishes a sense of continuity in thought. It is the dynamics of such categorizations and recategorizations that give our mental life the sense of a whole for which Freud postulates the existence of an unconscious. Specific unconscious memories would not account for a sense of continuity; continuity is a consequence of our ability to view things in larger relations, given the present.

In fact, in his early arguments against localization of function Freud appeared to stress these very points. As early as 1891, in his little-known book *On Aphasia*, Freud had argued that an idea cannot be separated from its associations. Freud considered illusory the evidence from brain-damaged subjects suggesting that concepts are "divided up" within the brain. The bits and pieces of a "concept" and its "associations" found in a brain-damaged patient are hardly bits and pieces: they are *different* concepts, new arrangements of information necessitated by the loss of brain tissue. Indeed, one cannot assume that brain damage destroys some mechanisms and spares others, and that clinical material will therefore reveal some of the brain's procedures stripped bare. "From the psychological point of view," Freud wrote, "we recognized the word as a complex of concepts (impressions, images) which through its sensory part (its auditory component) is connected with the complex of object associations."[48] The problem is hardly explained by localization of function, which implies the existence of stable "perceptions" and memories that are being "associated" with other perceptions and memories. A memory is the entire complex of ideas, and any new arrangement changes the ideas themselves. Or, to go beyond Freud, a memory is a generalization, or a categorization:

Is it possible [Freud asked in 1891], then, to differentiate the part of "perception" from that of "association" in the concomitant physiological process? Obviously not. *"Perception" and "association" are terms by which we describe different aspects of the same process. But we know that the phenomena to which these terms refer are abstractions from a unitary and indivisible process.* We cannot have a perception without immediately associating it; however sharply we may separate the two concepts, in reality they belong to one single process which, starting from one point, spreads over the whole cortex. The localization of the physiological correlates for perception and association is, therefore, identical and as localization of a perception means nothing else but localization of its correlate, we cannot possibly have a separate cortical localization for each.

Both arise from the same place and are nowhere static.[49] [Italics added.]

Past and present are inextricably intertwined. Freud believed in fixed memories, though the whole thrust of his observations and theory suggests the unreliability of recollection, and hence that memories themselves may not be fixed. "And when the obsessional patient lays his finger on the weak spot in the security of our mental life—on the untrustworthiness of our memory—the discovery enables him to extend his doubt over everything, even over actions which have already been performed . . . and over the entire past."[50]

Accurate memory traces would hardly help us survive in an ever-changing world. Freud attempted to account for how what he believed to be permanent memory traces could be altered in given circumstances. Yet, he often pinpointed the ways in which memories are new creations. Obsessional neurotics, for example, "redo" unpleasant experiences in a variety of obsessional rituals. Such rituals are memories *par excellence*—new creations, the past reworked—doomed to failure as *pleasant* corrections of the past because they are driven by *unpleasant* feelings, and hence the sought-after agreeable sensations remain elusive. That the rituals are generally composed of physical acts—"blowing away" the undesirable recollection, not so much in a symbolic way, as is often claimed, but in a very real attempt to redo, to create, a memory—points to the deep relation between movement and memory.

In a sense, all acts of recognition, all acts of recollection, require some kind of motor activity. We come to perceive and understand the physical world by exploring it with our hands, our eyes, and the movements of our bodies; our recollections and recognitions of the world are intimately related to those very movements we use to explore it. Motor acts help establish a context, an immediate contact with the environment.

In fact, we are all "redoing" the past, and an act of repetition must be understood not as an act symbolizing a specific past event but rather as a whole history of attempts at recapturing the past, a history that is being put into a specific context at a given moment when the repetition is occurring. A motorist hits the brakes when seeing a child dart into the middle of the street. Over the years the motorist has applied the brakes in similar circumstances, and the present act is related to all the previous ones, though it would be misleading to claim that there is a specific memory in the motorist's past that the act represents. Just as it would be misleading to say that a pianist's rendition of a sonata is a recollection of an earlier performance. Every performance is unique, though every performance does have a history; but the significance of that history depends on present context. When Freud compares *isolation* of a recollection in obsessional neurosis to amnesia (forgetting) in hysteria, he is making a profound observation about the nature of memory itself, for he is saying there is no recollection without context. And since context must, of necessity, constantly change, there can never be a fixed, or absolute, memory. Memory without the present cannot exist.

Against Localization

A Literary Interlude: Marcel Proust and Lost Time

Much as Freud believed that there is a "primal scene" that, through analysis, can suddenly be reawakened in a person's memory, Marcel Proust thought that memories can be elicited by such incidental sensations as uneven pavements (recalling to him his visit to Venice), starched napkins (his stay at Balbec), or the famous taste of the madeleine (his childhood in Combray):

Remembering with what relative indifference Swann years ago had been able to speak of the days when he had been loved, because what he saw beneath that phrase was not in fact those days but something else, and on the other hand the sudden pain which he had been caused by the little phrase of Vinteuil when it gave him back the days themselves just as they were when he had felt them in the past, I understood clearly that what the sensation of the uneven paving-stones, the stiffness of the napkin, the taste of the madeleine had reawakened in me had no connection with what I frequently tried to recall to myself of Venice, Balbec, Combray, with the help of an undifferentiated memory; and I understood that the reason why life may be judged to be trivial although at certain moments it seems to us so beautiful is that we form our judgment, ordinarily, on the evidence not of life itself but of those quite different images which preserve nothing of life—and therefore we judge it disparagingly.[51]*

*In the original:

Me rappelant trop avec quelle indifférence relative Swann avait pu parler autrefois des jours où il était aimé, parce que sous cette phrase il voyait autre chose qu'eux, et la douleur subite que lui avait causée la petite phrase de Vinteuil en lui rendant ces jours eux-mêmes, tels qu'il les avait jadis sentis, je comprenais trop que ce que la sensation des dalles inégales, la raideur de la serviette, le goût de la madeleine avaient réveillé en moi, n'avait aucun rapport avec ce que je cherchais souvent à me rappeler de Venise, de Balbec,

Yet, even these "pure" recollections of Proust's are a mixture of past and present.

And this cause I began to divine as I compared these diverse happy impressions, diverse yet with this in common, that I experienced them at the present moment and at the same time in the context of a distant moment, *so that the past was made to encroach upon the present and I was made to doubt whether I was in the one or the other.* The truth surely was that the being within me which had enjoyed these impressions had enjoyed them because they had in them something that was common to a day long past and to now, because in some way they were extra-temporal, and this being made its appearance only when, through one of these identifications of the present with the past, it was likely to find itself in the one and only medium in which it could exist and enjoy the essence of things, that is to say: outside time.* [Italics added.]

The past and the present have somehow become inter-twined into a more "real," vivid recollection. Proust at-tributes much importance to these "involuntary" recol-lections—they transcend any temporal relation—and associates them with a sense of great joy or happiness, suggesting that they encapsulate the satisfaction of deep needs and desires; as Freud's patients feel a sudden sense of relief and understanding when the primal scene

---

de Combray, à l'aide d'une mémoire uniforme; et je comprenais que la vie pût être jugée médiocre, bien qu'à certains moments elle parût si belle, parce que dans le premier cas c'est sur tout autre chose qu'elle-même, sur des images qui ne gardent rien d'elle, qu'on la juge et qu'on la déprécie.[52]

*Or cette cause, je la devinais en comparant ces diverse impressions bien-heureuses et qui avaient entre elles ceci de commun que je les éprouvais à la fois dans le moment actuel et dans un moment éloigné, *jusqu'à faire empiéter le passé sur le présent, à me faire hésiter à savoir dans lequel des deux je me trouvais;* au vrai, l'être qui alors goûtait en moi cette impression la goûtait en ce qu'elle avait de commun dans un jour ancien et maintenant, dans ce qu'elle avait d'extra-temporel, un être qui n'apparaissait que quand, par une de ces iden-tités entre le présent et le passé, il pouvait se trouver dans le seul milieu ou il pût vivre, jouir de l'essence des choses, c'est-à-dire en dehors du temps. [Italics added.]

becomes meaningful for them. These recollections, then, the primal scene in Freud and the involuntary memory in Proust, are more than vivid imaginations of the past. They represent a categorization, a generalization ("something that was common to a day long past and to now") of past and present events colored by a common emotional reaction. And because of subsequent events in either the patient's or Proust's life, these recollections *now* have a new meaning and therefore are not really the past events in themselves vividly recalled. They are different in both their emotional and intellectual significance for the individual.

Hence our perceptions of others and of things vary from moment to moment, "just as a feature in a landscape, a hill or a large country house, by appearing now on the right hand and now on the left and seeming first to dominate a forest and then to emerge from a valley, reveals to a traveller the changes in direction and the differences in altitude of the road along which he is passing."* So, too, our recollections of events depend on the perspective from which we view them.

A sense of mental continuity requires, Freud believed, the assumption of an unconscious that could store memories and that could respond to a variety of signals generated by the needs and desires of the individual. Yet the memories themselves are generalizations that are constantly being "revised." For Proust, continuity—a sense of being that transcended the minute-to-minute and day-to-day changes and transformations imposed by time—was established by kaleidoscoping two events, distant in time, place, and reference (the sound of a spoon

*"Comme un accident de terrain, colline ou château, qui apparait tantôt à droite, tantôt à gauche, semble d'abord dominer une forêt, ensuite sortir d'une vallée, et révèle ainsi au voyageur des changements d'orientation et des différences d'altitude dans la route qu'il suit."

and the sound of a hammer hitting the wheels of a train), into one timeless "recollection." But again, like Freud, Proust is describing the ways in which we create and recreate our categorizations of events, people, and things—the ways in which we constantly update our generalizations about the world. We learn to relate the differing views of a landscape to a particular place, or the different impressions of a close friend, moment to moment, with the same individual; so, too, our "past," what we take to be a collection of recollections, is really a new creation, an impression, that is related to the actual events and impressions of the past in the same way that our notion of the landscape is related to the variety of views—no single view being adequate to a full understanding of the landscape—from which we have, at any moment, generalized. If we are to understand brain function and its relation to psychology, we must explain this extraordinary capacity to generalize and categorize the people and things about us.

Localization of Function Today: The Brain as a Collection of Functionally Specialized Units

Many, if not most, psychologists and neuroscientists today are convinced that the brain consists of individual functional units—called *modules*—that may or may not be anatomically localized. In England, John C. Marshall and Freda Newcombe published a series of papers beginning in 1966 in which they explained reading difficulties in brain-damaged patients as an inability to retrieve from memory specific aspects of a word, such as its pronunciation or its meaning. They argued that such incapacities helped psychologists understand brain function since, in their view, brain damage causes the loss of specific functions while sparing others. Similarly, in the 1970s Elizabeth Warrington tried to show how specific brain lesions cause the loss of limited categories of information, again assuming that the brain has, at least functionally, discretely organized memory centers. Curiously, an interesting but unheeded study of aphasia published in 1931 (and referred to by Marshall and Newcombe) had already suggested why these approaches might be wrong.

Context and Meaning: A. A. Low and A. R. Luria

In 1930, the Chicago physician A. A. Low treated a patient who had suffered a cerebrovascular accident the previous year with a consequent partial paralysis and loss of speech. By November 1929, he had recovered his capacity to speak "in well formed sentences, though with some difficulty in finding words." But his recovery was marred by a peculiar, though limited, handicap: "When given a sentence or paragraph to read . . . , he left out many words and combinations of words, giving the distinct impression of agrammatical reading." In the course of the following months, Low attempted to pinpoint the nature of the defect and its cause. Initially, he showed the patient lists of concrete nouns like *dad*, *child*, and *shirt*. Some nouns, such as *dad*, were read as "father." The patient apparently understood the word but failed to recognize the actual printed version. Other examples of similar mistakes were "girl" for *child* and "wicked" for *vice*. The patient also made what were probably visual errors, such as "skirt" for *shirt*. [53]

Then he was shown sixty verbs in groups of ten infinitives (*to go, to quit,* and so on); ten past tenses (*registered, organized,* and so on); ten present tenses *(tells, goes)*; ten participles *(fleeing, fishing)*; ten imperatives *(go, hear)*; and ten past tenses of irregular verbs *(lost, torn)*. He read the imperatives and the past tenses of irregular verbs correctly, but he read infinitives without the *to* ("speed" instead of *to speed*) and present-tense verbs without the proper endings ("go" for *goes*) or participles ("flee" instead of *fleeing*). He tended to drop affixes (flee-*ing*, go-*es*).*

Having noticed a tendency in the patient to drop the final *s* on the plural form of nouns, Low tested his ability to read combinations such as "many houses" and "six brothers." The patient read these short phrases correctly. "The fact," Low concluded, "that in three separate performances not one confusion of plural and singular occurred was taken as indisputable evidence that the patient had a considerable facility for handling singular and plural, and the mistakes observed in the preceding tests referred to a tendency to leave out affixes, not to an ignorance of grammar." [54] Further testing showed an almost total inability to read short function words such as *at, to, as,* and *in,* though the patient had relatively less difficulty with longer function words such as *beyond, above,* and *beneath.* Low concluded that length was not the problem: long and short particles differed radically with regard to their reference to meaning. Words like *at* and *as* have a range of meanings (at home, at ease, at your service)

---

*Past tenses of irregular verbs and imperatives do not have affixes *(lost, torn, go)*.

and acquire a specific sense only in a given context. On the other hand, words like *beyond* and *above* have definite meanings of their own, regardless of context.

Low argued that his patient's abilities were limited because he was wholly dependent on meaning when reading—as became particularly evident when Low gave him nonsense syllables like *lem, sim, fik,* or *tek* to read. Trying to make sense of these nonsense syllables, he read *sto,* for example, as "story," *fal* as "fat," *ser* as "serve," and *tla* as "atlas." He also had considerable difficulty with symbols (for example: $) and abbreviations (U.S., G.O.P.). He even had difficulty with individual letters of the alphabet, reading *J* as "John" and Low's name *A. A. Low, M.D.,* as "Low, doctor of medicine." Function words in a context, however ("clear as mud," "off guard"), gave him little difficulty. This need to "understand" written material was again evident when Low gave his patient short sentences to read, among them, "France builds ships"; "Children play games"; "Waiters serve food." When some of these same words were used in nonsense sentences ("Serve booksellers books"; "Play waiters food"; "Make, stop, listen"), his patient would misread the sentences ("Waiters sell food"; "Stop, look, and listen") in an apparent attempt to give a coherent meaning to the collections of words. Sentences with numbers and function words like *each* or *a*—specifying a grammatical function or relation between words— gave the patient considerable difficulty.[55]

Further testing, however, revealed that the patient's apparent inability to understand function words, such as *above* and *below,* was not total. When asked to hold a pencil above, or a match below, the table, he was unable to carry out either order. But when asked to "hold the pencil above his head or below his chin, or to put the watch on his nose or to hold it between his eyes, he performed well." Orders such as "show your nose" or "raise your leg" were promptly carried out; but when the examiner said, "Touch my chair," the patient became confused. He could understand spatial relations in terms of his own body but not in terms of external objects. He had no difficulty, however, manipulating objects or identifying them manually.[56]

Changes of context, then, can profoundly alter a brain-damaged patient's ability to understand and use language. Nonetheless, psychologists today often test patients with lists of words and pictures, ignoring problems of context, and conclude that the failure to identify individual words or images is evidence of a specific memory loss.

Yet, in the 1960s, A. R. Luria described a patient with a remarkable memory who created artificial contexts in order to remember (and to forget!) random lists of words. In *The Mind of a Mnemonist,* Luria recounted how his patient used the device of an imaginary map of a small town to recall the lists. He placed each word at a different location and would then *perceive* the list as a part of the map. Failures to remember a particular word, Luria notes, were not

defects of memory . . . but were, in fact, *defects of perception.* [Such memory slips] could not be explained in terms of established ideas on the neurodynamics of memory traces (retroactive and proactive inhibition, extinction of traces, etc.) but rather by certain factors that influence perception (clarity, contrast, the ability to isolate a figure from its background, the degree of lighting available, etc.). His errors could not be explained, then, in terms of the psychology of memory but had to do with the psychological factors that govern perception. . . .

"I put the image of the *pencil* near a fence [Luria's patient explained] . . . the one down the street, you know. But what happened was that the image fused with that of the fence and I walked right on past without noticing it. The same thing happened with the word *egg*. I had put it up against a white wall and it blended in with the background. How could I possibly spot a white egg up against a white wall? Now take the word *blimp*. That's something grey, so it blended in with the grey of the pavement . . . *banner*, of course, means the Red Banner. But, you know, the building which houses the Moscow City Soviet Workers' Deputies is also red, and since I'd put the banner close to one of the walls of the building I just walked on without seeing it."[57]

The mnemonist "forgot" what he was unable to *recognize* in his imaginary landscape. Unlike the perceptual difficulties of the patients of Giraudeau, Dejerine, and others, the mnemonist's perceptual problem was a consequence of an inappropriately *chosen* background (context). But what emerges from all these studies is that recollection is a kind of perception, and that therefore every context will alter the nature of what is recalled.

Three Routes in Reading: John C. Marshall and Freda Newcombe

In spite of Freud, in spite of Low, in spite of Luria, the assumed principles of brain function have hardly changed, though the relatively simple diagrams of Wernicke and Lichtheim have become more complicated. For example, the Oxford psychologists John Marshall and Freda Newcombe—whose own case work, as they have acknowledged, is strikingly similar to Low's 1931 case study—present a model of reading in which they distinguish three "routes" that the brain may use to assign a linguistic structure to visualized written words: a route based on the sound of words (the *phonetic* route); a route based on seeing the word as a unit (the *direct* route); and a route based on the meaning of words (the *lexical* route). Marshall and Newcombe's work with brain-damaged patients purports to show why confusions about meaning arise when the various routes are not in perfect order. As Marshall explained their position in 1985:

The position advanced by Marshall and Newcombe (1973) was essentially a revival of the theoretical approach (and notational conventions) that the early diagram-makers (Lichtheim, 1885) had adopted in the analysis of aphasic impairment. An account of normal reading was proposed whereby multiple routes operated, largely in parallel, to assign form, sound, and meaning to the written word. The model was expressed as a (very simple) flow diagram; boxes indicated processing stages where distinct linguistic representations are assigned to their input; arrows showed the flow of information between processing stages [see figure 1.5]. It was then conjectured that the individual components of this normal functional architecture could each be independently destroyed or impaired by brain damage. The resultant performance would thus in part follow from the *normal* operation of the remaining intact "boxes and arrows"; symptomatology that could not be so interpreted would be consequent upon principled restrictions or perturbations of defined processing stages.[58]

For example, Marshall and Newcombe argue that some patients can read words only phonetically (the phonetic route). One brain-damaged war veteran interpreted the word *listen* as a reference to the boxing champion Sonny Liston. *Billed,* which he read correctly, he thought meant "build." Spelling failed to give this patient the essential clues about the different meanings of homonyms: he read the word *pair* correctly and remarked, "It's either two of a kind or it's the one for eating. I don't know which." And pronouncing the *s* in

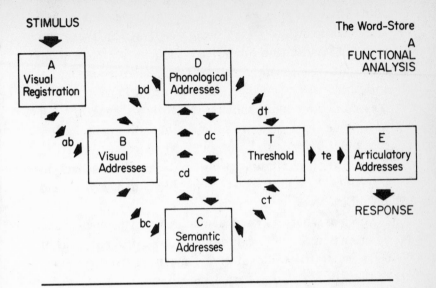

Figure 1.5.

The 1973 Marshall-Newcombe schema for reading aloud. In the figure "functional components are labeled with capital letters, functional relationships are labeled with pairs of small letters, whose order indicates the direction of the relationship. The figure illustrates that, in reading individual words, visual addresses (B) must be associated with stimulus entries on a primary visual register; that both phonological (D) and semantic (C) addresses must in turn be associated with individual visual addresses; and that for 'word-perception' to occur, the 'value' of the pair CD must exceed a certain threshold. Given that value, the lexical entry may then be associated with an articulatory address which determines the final response." Note that the illustrated schema has only two routes, and in the text a three-route schema is discussed.
SOURCE: John C. Marshall and Freda Newcombe, "Patterns of Paralexia: A Psycholinguistic Approach," *Journal of Psycholinguistic Research* 2, no. 3 (1973): 189. (Quote from page 188.)

island, he concluded, "It doesn't mean anything. . . . There's no such word."[59]

By contrast, brain-damaged patients who used what Marshall and Newcombe call the lexical route for analyzing words showed an ability to comprehend words without being able to read them aloud. Marshall and Newcombe give the following examples: *sick* was read as "ill"; *bush* as "tree"; *act* as "play"; *ancient* as "historic"; and *tall* as "long." Some of these difficulties are similar to a child's tendency to overgeneralize (see page 102), as in the case of the patient who read *chair* as "table" and *down* as "up." By these examples, Marshall and Newcombe meant to show how, with the breakdown of specific functional units—their "routes"—one's understanding of words and sentences may become abnormal. Yet normal people will probably find some "sense" in these linguistic failings—for example, when *chair* is read as "table."

Much of what we observe in language disorders caused by brain damage, the argument claims, is probably part of the normal process for deriving meaning from symbols, words, and visual information. Because some mechanisms are destroyed or disconnected, the brain has less of a choice in establishing suitable meanings in a given situation. Thus, Marshall and Newcombe argued:

We may logically hypothesize that the process of reading an individual word (with understanding) involves the retrieval of the full lexical entry associated with the particular visual stimulus. Katz and Fodor suggest that the normal form for dictionary entries should be . . .

BUSH
noun
(plant)
(with branches)
[arising from or near the ground]

The entry is characterized by a part of speech classification, by a (set of) SEMANTIC MARKERS (enclosed in parentheses) which indicate those general properties of the semantic structure of the language instanced by the word, and by a DISTINGUISHER (enclosed in a square bracket) which indicates whatever is idiosyncratic about the meaning of the lexical item. The process of reading aloud may thus be seen as retrieving the full dictionary entry associated with the visual configuration and encoding this specification into the appropriate phonological form. As the patient we have described has very little difficulty in "understanding" language, what we are apparently seeing in this case is a breakdown of the encoding process. The patient reads BUSH as "tree" having thus encoded the lexical entry as far as the distinguisher (i.e., the phonological shape corresponding to "noun" + (plant) + (with branches) is "tree").

When either of two phonological shapes may be appropriately associated with a given dictionary entry the patient may select the wrong one, that is, he produces a "pure" synonym (e.g., ILL read as "sick"). Sometimes he may only succeed in encoding the form class of the stimulus. He reads UP as "and," thus encoding a very primitive "function-word" marker. (Although the patient cannot read prepositions aloud he had no difficulty in correctly selecting pictures on the basis of descriptions containing prepositions. Given, for example, the sentence "The cup is under the table" he could point to the correct picture of a pair with a cup under and on the table.)[60]

Like much contemporary psychological work, these studies have ignored the effect of context. After all, Marshall and Newcombe's parenthetical remark in the passage just cited—noting that the patient "cannot read prepositions aloud" but had "no difficulty in correctly selecting pictures on the basis of descriptions containing prepositions"—is a perfect description of how context can alter recognition: isolated prepositions may be unrecognizable, but given a context (a sentence), they can be instantly recognized.

Context and Categorization: Elizabeth Warrington

Though she, too, believes that brain function is divided into various specialized units, the English psychologist Elizabeth Warrington has suggested that the patterns of breakdowns found in some aphasics may be due to a memory loss of categories of things, ideas, and so on. For example, it is relatively common to find patients who, like Low's, retain knowledge of concrete nouns (given a noun such as *table*, they will point to a picture of a table) and yet are not able to understand abstract nouns (like *aptitude*). Warrington, on the other hand, has described cases of patients who have lost concrete nouns but could still identify those that are abstract. One patient, when asked to define *hay*, responded, "I've forgotten"; and when asked to define *poster*, said, "No idea." Yet given the word *supplication*, he said, "making a serious request for help," and *pact*, "friendly agreement."[61]

In related work, Warrington and Tim Shallice studied four patients who showed "a significant discrepancy between their ability to identify inanimate objects and [their] inability to identify living things and food." Incorrect identifications included *crocus* as "rubbish material" and *spider* as "person looking for things, he was a spider for a nation"; the same patient could readily "define" *umbrella*: "object used to protect you from water that comes," or *towel*: "material used to dry people."[62] Warrington analyzed this kind of evidence as follows:

If one accepts the evidence of category specificity, the significance of these unexpected dissociations within the broad domain of concrete words is of some theoretical interest. They are unlikely to be arbitrary. Their occurrence leads one once again to infer not only that the neural substrates of these categories are different, but that they are required to be different for efficient access to their semantic representations. Living things and man-made objects are alike in so far as both are tangible things that can be allocated to a hierarchy of superordinate categories but they differ in so far as living things are comprehended in terms of attributes or distinguishing features that differentiate them from other similar members of the same class. Perhaps this applies to foods as well. On the other hand, objects are comprehended not only in terms of physical properties but also in terms of *function*. I would speculate that it is the paramount importance of function, as compared with physical attributes, which require separate mechanisms to achieve their respective semantic representations.[63]

But one suspects a larger possibility is being overlooked. For Warrington's categories may emerge as a consequence of the limitations imposed on the damaged brain's power to generalize. It is not necessarily specific categories, but certain powers of generalization, that are being lost. Generalization—or categorization in this larger sense—cannot be explained in terms of "semantic representation[s] of verbal concepts [that] are structured in a definite order or hierarchy."[64]

Ultimately, Warrington's categories, like Marshall and Newcombe's routes, are but aids to a filing system that these psychologists appear to consider an essential element of brain function. Yet no filing system can account for the extraordinary variety of ways in which we can parcel up the world, any more than a filing system could store the innumerable patterns of muscular coordination that we use from one occasion to another in writing and speaking identical words and phrases. And just as our ability to produce language cannot be accounted for in these terms, neither can our ability to recognize words and sentences. For, as discussed in part 2, the linguistic signs we "hear"—the words and sentences that make up everyday speech—are abstractions, created by our brains, of the actual acoustic structures of language. The formation of such abstractions (the categorizations of stimuli), the fact that their meanings depend on context and are not absolute, appear to be characteristic of brain function in general. And it is the brain's categorization—categorization not in Warrington's sense, but categorization as generalization—of a variety of visual and auditory cues into linguistic "gestural patterns" that is essential to our recognition of speech.

Indeed, just as the sounds we associate with language, the sounds we "think" we actually hear, are abstractions (categorizations or generalizations of linguistic "gestures"), so too syntax and ultimately meaning may also be higher abstractions of sets of gestural patterns. The basis of syntax may be phonetic; and rules of grammar may have little to do with the way syntactic structures emerge in the brain. Our understanding of the gestural nature of speech probably derives from work that dates back to the first attempts to reproduce speech mechanically, and it is to that story that we now turn.

2

Language as Gesture
and the Recognition
of Speech

> All the psychological schools and trends over-
> look the cardinal point that every thought is a
> generalization; and they all study word and
> meaning without any reference to development.
> —LEV SEMENOVICH VYGOTSKY,
> *Thought and Language* (1934)

IN 1779, the Imperial Academy of St. Petersburg offered a prize for the solution to the following questions:
"What is the nature and character of the sounds of the
vowels *a, e, i, o, u* that make them so different from one
another? Can an instrument be constructed like the *vox
humana* pipes of an organ, which shall accurately express
the sounds of the vowels?" Christian Gottlieb Kratzenstein won the prize for a set of acoustic resonators that
were similar in size to the human mouth and varied in

form with the particular vowel desired (see figure 2.1). Kratzenstein activated his resonators with a vibrating reed that imitated the action of the vocal cords. Five vowels, it was claimed, were reproduced "with tolerable accuracy."

A more successful machine was built in 1791 by Wolfgang von Kempelen of Vienna. Apparently von Kempelen's reputation in scientific circles had been badly damaged when it was learned that an early invention of his, a chess-playing "machine" which had won many games, had hidden within it a legless officer of the Polish army, a master chess player named Worouski. Von Kempelen's speaking machine was considerably more ingenious and contained no little man. A stream of air from a bellows was forced across a reed, causing it to vibrate, and then passed through a hand-held leather resonator whose shape could be altered by the hand until acceptable vowel sounds were produced. Consonants such as *s* and *sh* were produced by constricting the passage to the

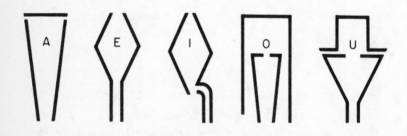

Figure 2.1.

Kratzenstein's acoustic resonators, 1779. Air was blown over a reed placed at the bottom of the individual resonators, and the indicated vowel sounds were produced.

SOURCE: James L. Flanagan, "The Synthesis of Speech," *Scientific American* (February 1972): 52. Copyright © 1972 by Scientific American, Inc. All rights reserved.

resonator with a series of levers controlled by the other hand (see figure 2.2). Among those impressed by this device was the Scottish-born Alexander Graham Bell, who as a boy in Edinburgh had built with his brother a simulation of the human vocal apparatus which could produce a few simple words.

Recognizable voice sounds can, therefore, be produced mechanically as groups of articulatory gestures. And since the set of movements that produce the vocal sound can be visually observed, the intended vocal sound can be recognized visually without being heard. So, too, lip reading is, in principle, possible through observation of movements of the lip, jaw, and so on. There will be an inevitable ambiguity, since we cannot observe *all* the articulatory movements of the vocal tract used to produce a given sound, as we can with von Kempelen's machine.

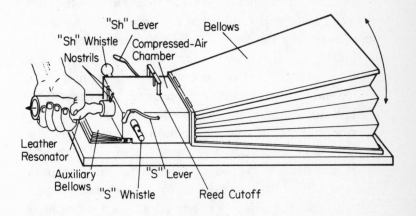

Figure 2.2.

Von Kempelen's speaking machine, 1791. The bellows is used to blow air over a reed and then in turn through the hand-controlled leather resonator. Other vocal sounds were imitated using the additional constricted passages.

SOURCE: James L. Flanagan, "The Synthesis of Speech," *Scientific American* (February 1972): 52. Copyright © 1972 by Scientific American, Inc. All rights reserved.

Nonetheless, lip reading is possible, and in the past it was assumed that those who had mastered the art had learned to associate particular vocal sounds with various positions of the lips, jaws, and so on. That this was false became evident in 1976 when the English psychologists Harry McGurk and John MacDonald described experiments in which subjects saw but did not hear a person talking on a screen. The person on the screen silently articulated, for example, the sounds /ga/ga/, while an offscreen voice said /ba/ba/. The subjects actually heard /da/da/. If they turned away from the screen, they heard /ba/ba/. Though the subjects knew what was happening, they could not avoid this auditory "illusion." In a variation of the McGurk-MacDonald experiment, the person on the silent screen articulated /dee/dee/dee/, while an offscreen voice said /ba/ba/ba/. The subjects actually heard /da/da/da/, taking their cue, for the consonant, from the lip and facial gestures they saw on the screen and, for the vowel, from the taped voice.

Indeed, children acquire languages by generalizing about a variety of spoken and visual cues. At first, they notice the grosser aspects of speech that carry meaning, though individual words and sentences may not be understood. Some infants, for example, at first mimic the variations in intonation and emphasis of adult speech. They may become so good at imitating the different intonations that adults think the infants are speaking actual sentences, though in fact the syllables do not comprise real words. Evidently, the sense, or meaning, the adult is trying to convey is, for the infant, in the prosodic contours of sound. "A child's entry into language is mediated by meaning . . . [and its] earliest unit of meaning is probably the prosodic contour: the rising pitch of question and surprise, the falling pitch of declaration, and so on, often observed in stretches of 'jargon' or intonated babble."[1]

Intonational mimicry is followed by the acquisition of both syllables and the phonetic segments (consonants and vowels) of which syllables are composed.

But neither syllables nor segments are immediately given to the child. Instead, they gradually emerge as the child comes to master their component articulatory gestures. We see this quite clearly when we notice . . . that individual words may vary widely in their phonetic form from one occasion to another. A striking example comes from Ferguson and Farwell. They report ten radically different attempts by a 15-month-old girl, K, to say *pen* within one half-hour session. . . . On the surface, these attempts seem almost incomprehensibly diverse one from another and from their model. But the authors shrewdly remark that 'K seems to be trying to sort out the features of nasality, bilabial closure, alveolar closure, and voicelessness.' . . . An alternative description . . . would be to say that all the *gestures* of the model (lip closure, tongue raising and fronting, alveolar closure, velum lowering/raising, glottal opening/closing) are to be found in one or other of these utterances, but that the gestures are incorrectly phased with respect to one another. Thus, the adult model evidently specified for the child the required gestures, but not their relative timing.[2]

Apparently the child recognizes speech sounds as *patterns of gestures* and, in attempting to reproduce them, often fails to produce the correct sound because of an error in timing. The child's initial recognitions are of the larger contours, and the exact timing in the sequencing of gestures is not reproduced, even if it is noticed. As the child acquires a greater sensitivity to timing, however, it becomes important in recognition as well. Initially, the detailed organization and the ways in which it varies from one utterance to another are not sufficiently grasped. But what is striking is that children establish categories of gestures that they perceive as important in adult speech and try to imitate word production using these categories. Eventually a pattern of gestures, a set of articulatory movements, becomes a categorization for a specific phoneme, or unit of sound.

Thus the significance of a set of gestures follows a sequence from the general to the specific (infants first acquire general abilities to imitate intonations), and the pattern of general to specific occurs in the acquisition of meaning as well. The psychologist Breyne Arlene Moskowitz observed one child who quickly generalized the word *clock*, learned in reference to a particular object, to encompass all round objects, such as gas meters and bathroom scales. Other children did not distinguish between pairs of words such as *before/after* and *more/less*. As Moskowitz wrote, "children acquire first the part of the meaning that is common to both words and only later the part of the meaning that distinguishes the two."[3] In a larger sense, one could argue that the significance of any linguistic structure is in a constant state of flux throughout an individual's lifetime.

The Perception of Speech

Our *perceptions* of the sound structures of language, then, depend on our recognition of "a coordinated pattern of gestures."[4] The sound structures essential to communication—the vowels and consonants of a language—are perceptual generalizations of a variety of acoustic and visual cues that emerge over time. The gestures marshaled for the production of a specific phoneme, however, are not invariant. Rather, the required gestures depend on the *combination* of sounds one wants to produce, as well as on requirements of emphasis, desired quality of voice (for example, serious, mocking), and so on. The significance of a particular gesture—like the significance of a letter in isolation—cannot be determined unambiguously.

This concept was demonstrated in work inspired largely by Alvin Liberman and done at the Haskins Laboratories (now in New Haven) beginning in the 1940s.[5] Liberman and his colleagues used a wave-analyzing device that converted speech patterns into a visual display known as a *spectrogram*. Using the spectrogram as a model, the group painted, on clear celluloid sheets, simplified patterns that were converted to sound by having light projected through them (see figure 2.3). The instrument was called a "pattern playback."

Through a series of trials and errors, the group isolated essential cues that produced synthetic sounds but intelligible speech. Spectrograms of vowel sounds showed several dark areas of fairly constant frequencies called *formants*. Different frequency patterns were, in general, associated with different vowels. Finding that three, and even as few as two, formants were sufficient to allow listeners to identify the six vowels in English, the Haskins researchers traced on the celluloid sheet of the pattern playback thick lines that corresponded to the appropriate frequencies of the essential formants of a given vowel. Furthermore, by varying the frequency of the initial part of a formant (moving rapidly from a

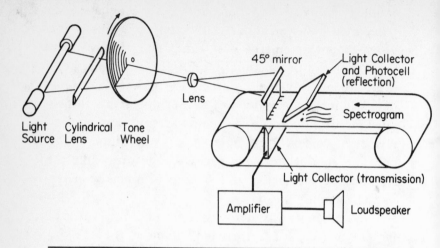

Figure 2.3.

The pattern playback. Using light, a spectrogram (which plots how the frequency and amplitude of vocal sounds change over time) is converted into sound. Liberman and his colleagues painted stylized copies of the spectrograms of many different utterances, deleted or pruned parts, and converted these simplified patterns into sound on the pattern playback.

SOURCE: Alvin L. Liberman, Pierre Delatte, and Franklin S. Cooper, "The Role of Selected Stimulus-Variables in the Perception of the Unvoiced Stop Consonants," *American Journal of Psychology* 45, no. 4 (October 1952): 501.

lower to a higher frequency, or from a higher to a lower frequency), a consonant sound is heard before the vowel. The varying portion of the formant is called a *formant transition* and, when heard in isolation, it sounds like chirping. When combined with the vowel formants, no chirping sound is heard, as was dramatically demonstrated in experiments in which two formants (the first and second formants with their associated formant transitions) were presented to one ear and the isolated third-formant transition to the other ear. By themselves the first and second formants with their formant transitions were heard by most listeners as the syllable *da*, though some heard it as *ga* (see figure 2.4).The isolated third-

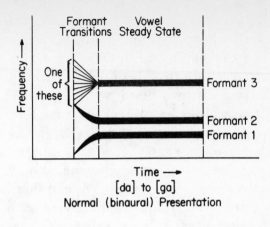

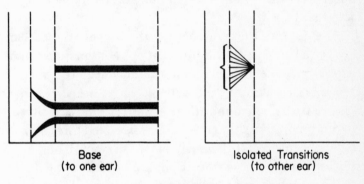

Figure 2.4.

The dichotic listening experiment. Note that the third-formant transition (illustrated as any one of the possible transitions in the lower left-hand diagram) is heard as a chirping sound in isolation. When combined with the formants and formant transitions represented in the lower left-hand diagram, a *da* or *ga,* but no chirping sound, is heard. Therefore, context determines how the rapidly changing frequency of the chirping sound, or the transition formant, is perceived.

SOURCE: A. M. Liberman, "On Finding That Speech Is Special," *American Psychologist* 37 (1982): 153. Copyright 1982 by the American Psychological Corporation. Reprinted by permission of the publisher and author.

formant transition (which normally determines, depending on its direction, whether a *d* or a *g* is heard) was heard as a chirping sound in the other ear. When the stimuli were presented to both ears simultaneously, the isolated transition was heard as a chirp in the ear to which it was presented and, at the same time, as the syllable *da* in the other ear (or *ga*, depending on the particular third formant). Sounds are categorized and therefore perceived differently depending on the presence or absence of other sounds. The chirping sound of a formant transition, readily heard when it is isolated, is not perceived when it is combined with other vocal sounds.

And just as the presence of the vowel sounds can change a chirping sound into that of a consonant, so, too, gaps of silence between sounds can affect the sounds heard. For example, the syllable *sa* is heard when a "noisy patch" of sound (the *s* sound) is followed by the two formant transitions and their associated formants, as seen in figure 2.5. If the noisy patch is removed and only the formants and the transitions are produced, a listener will generally hear *ta*. And if the noisy patch is played again, but a small stretch of silence (50 milliseconds) separates it from the onset of the formant transitions, a listener will hear *sta*.

So, too, if an interval of silence is introduced between the words *say* and *shop* in the phrase "say shop," listeners will hear "say chop." The silence has cued the closure of the vocal tract, implying an intended *ch* sound rather than a *sh* sound. The effect of the silence can be overcome by lengthening the *sh* sound in *shop*, so there is apparently a trade-off between the length of the *sh* sound and the duration of the silence in determining whether *sh* or *ch* is heard.

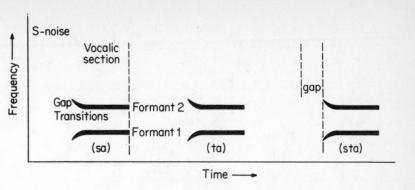

Figure 2.5.

Schematic spectrograms illustrating the importance of silence for the perception of a stop consonant: *sa* becomes *ta* when the noise is removed, or *sta* when a silent interval of appropriate length is introduced between the noise and the rest of the syllable.

SOURCE: A. M. Liberman and M. Studdert-Kennedy, "Phonetic Perception," in *Handbook of Sensory Physiology*, ed. R. Held, H. W. Leibowitz, and H.-L. Teuber, vol. 8, *Perception* (New York: Springer-Verlag, 1978), p. 158.

Lengthening the period of silence *between* words can also alter the *preceding* word. As in the previous experiment, increasing the period of silence between the words *gray* and *ship* made listeners hear "gray chip" rather than "gray ship," the increased silence signaling a closure of the vocal tract appropriate for the sound *ch* rather than *sh* (see figure 2.6). However, if the cue for the *sh* in "ship" is relatively long, increases in the duration of the silence between the words cause the perception to change, not to "gray chip" but to "great ship." The silence is still taken as a cue for closure of the vocal tract, but now the long *sh* sound in the second word causes the brain to attribute the closure to the *previous* syllable, changing *gray* to *great*, the *t* sound requiring closure of the vocal tract.

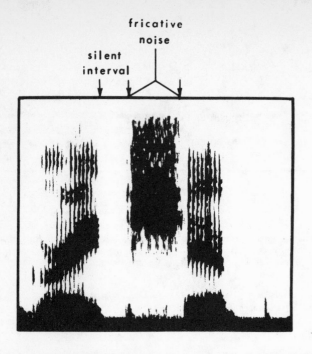

Figure 2.6.

Spectrogram of the words *gray ship*.
SOURCE: A. M. Liberman, "On Finding That Speech Is Special," *American Psychologist* 37 (1982): 163. Copyright 1982 by the American Psychological Association. Reprinted by permission of the publisher and author.

Furthermore, it is characteristic of speech that the cues for the different phonemes are delivered simultaneously. When uttering the word *bag* (see figure 2.7), a speaker begins shaping the tongue for the vowel sound *a* before completing the lip movement for the *b*. This coarticulation of the phonetic message permits rapid transmission, which would be impossible if each phoneme had to be articulated in turn. Not only do the cues for vowels and consonants overlap, but they vary accord-

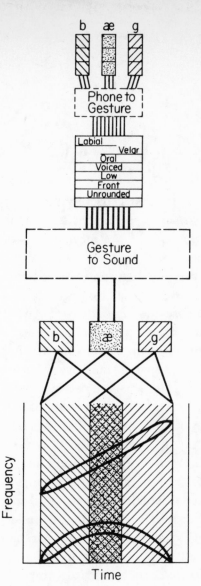

Frequency

Time

Figure 2.7.

Schematic diagram showing how the clues for the phonetic segments of the word *bag* overlap when the word is uttered. Note, for example, that the clues for *b* overlap with those for *æ* and *g*. In the upper part of the diagram, the various vocal gestures required for the different phonemes that make up the word *bag* are indicated. Not only do the gestures overlap, but a particular combination of vocal gestures is heard as one sound or another depending on what gestures precede and follow it. In other words, the particular linguistic sounds we hear, such as *b* or *æ*, are not absolutely determined by a given set of vocal gestures but are determined by the context—the preceding and following sounds—in which those gestures are made.

SOURCE: A. M. Liberman, "The Grammars of Speech and Language," *Cognitive Psychology* 1 (1970): 314.

ing to context. Changing the vowel in *bag* changes the cues for the *b* and the *g*.

Categorization, Not Localization

In what sense, then, can one say that a specific area of the brain or a specific brain *mechanism*, is responsible for the production of the phoneme /a/, if the mechanisms of production depend on the surrounding phonemes? What part of the brain, what brain mechanism, is responsible for our perceptions of an /a/, if what we perceive also depends on what came before and after the /a/? And if the perceptual mechanisms are such that a brief silence between the words *gray* and *chip* can result in our hearing *great ship*, how can we talk of a specific memory trace for *gray, chip, great,* or *ship*? For sure, what we perceive in all these examples depends on interrelating a variety of sensory cues (stimuli), and, at best, we can say that an *overall pattern of brain activity* must be responsible for these different perceptions. There is no word center in the brain. An interrelated pattern of activity among many brain "centers" causes us to perceive a given word in a given context. Only recently have we come to understand what brain "centers" are—and they are, as we shall see, very different from anything assumed in the nineteenth century or even in twentieth-century computer simulations.

The sounds that make up speech are, when heard individually, without import for us (for example, the chirping sound of the transition formants). But when placed in an appropriate context, they become a member of a group. We assign them to a category, so that they take on a linguistic function (as, for example, a phoneme). Of course, how this category is perceived depends on the categorizations of the preceding and following sounds as well. There are no absolute rules of categorization: it is a fluid process allowing us to form new categories. We must, for example, be able to categorize speech sounds in different ways when learning a new language, just as a child appears to alter his or her categorization of speech gestures with the acquisition of new words.

The categorizations created by our brains are abstract and cannot be accounted for as combinations of "elementary" stimuli. In the nineteenth century, Hermann von Helmholtz proposed that a given frequency of sound causes the vibration of specific fibers in the ear that are tuned to that frequency. In this theory, every frequency has a specific region of the brain responsible for its identification. Other brain centers would have to combine these "simple" stimuli into more complex sound patterns. Helmholtz himself was disturbed that his theory failed to explain the perception of consonance and dissonance. The model implied, too, that the perception of speech should be more difficult than that of pure musical tones. But, as N. A. Bernstein wrote in 1935,

a pure musical tone is simpler in its acoustic structure than the sounds of the human voice—vowels with their numerous formants, and consonants with their characteristic phonation. For a resonating harp [a device that would respond to sounds in a way that is analogous to Helmholtz's theory of individual frequency receptors in the ear] these can be recognized in no other way than by their analysis into simple components and only after the determination of these components; consequently, on this model the discrimination of speech sounds is more complicated than the discrimination of pure tones and is based entirely on the latter process. As far as the human organ of hearing is concerned, *many* people have musical (relative) discrimination while *all* understand and perceive speech. Very striking cases of tone deafness have been described. [Köhler, for example, described a patient who not only could] not understand what was meant by a melody, but was even unable to distinguish between a low and a high tone, while he could distinguish all shades of speech and accent very well, indeed, imitating provincial accents quite well in telling anecdotes (such persons have no physical defects of hearing).[6]

How we perceive stimuli depends on how they are categorized, how they are organized in terms of other stimuli, not on their absolute structure (such as the absolute frequency of a sound).

But how does the brain create the categories and generalizations that appear to be fundamental to its ability to make sense of the world without relying on any permanent memory images? In the early 1970s workers in artificial intelligence attempted to simulate various forms of behavior. They suggested that successful simulations of particular tasks might give important clues about how the brain achieves its goals. Fundamental to this approach is the assumption that acquired knowledge is stored as fixed images in specific centers, just as the nineteenth-century neurologists had believed. The images are given "addresses" in the computer models, in the same way as the nineteenth-century neurologists assigned them to specialized brain centers. The world is knowable, according to this view, only if it is already known: the recognition of a shape is possible only if there is a fixed image of that shape already stored somewhere in the brain.

In the mid-1970s, this approach was challenged by a

young English mathematician and neuroscientist named David Marr (1945–1980), who showed that shapes could be recognized as shapes, without any previous knowledge of them. Marr did not totally abandon the idea of fixed memories, since ultimately the *naming* of a shape required, in his scheme, a memory search. Nonetheless, the idea that shape recognition is possible by carrying out certain procedures (what computer scientists call "computations") on visual stimuli without any matching of stimuli to previously stored images suggested a profound new approach to memory. Marr may have failed to recognize in just what ways his work was truly innovative and what, from a biological standpoint, ultimately limited his approach. For Marr had discovered and described *one* example of memory as procedure—the kind of memory that Broca had first hinted at in his discussion of motor memory (see part I). Here was a concrete example of recognition without any fixed memory. Marr, however, never claimed that he was describing memory as such. But in retrospect, it is the description of memory as procedure that may well be Marr's greatest achievement.

PART

3

Machine Recognition

> After playing Chopin, I feel as if I had been weeping over sins that I had never committed, and mourning over tragedies that were not my own. Music always seems to me to produce that effect. It creates for one a past of which one has been ignorant, and fills one with a sense of sorrows that have been hidden from one's tears. I can fancy a man who had led a perfectly commonplace life, hearing by chance some curious piece of music, and suddenly discovering that his soul, without his being conscious of it, had passed through terrible experiences, and known fearful joys, or wild romantic loves, or great renunciations.
>
> —OSCAR WILDE, "The Critic as Artist" (1891)

DURING the 1950s, neurophysiologists discovered neurons (nerve cells) in the visual cortex that are activated by specific stimuli. Within the frog's brain they found detectors that fired whenever a moving convex object appeared in a specific part of the frog's visual field. If the object failed to move, or if it was of the wrong shape, the neuron would not fire: hungry frogs would not jump at dead flies hanging on a string, but would if the string was jiggled. In their studies of cat and monkey visual cortexes, David Hubel and Torsten Wiesel found neurons that were sensitive to lines and bars with specific horizontal, vertical, and oblique orientations. The visual cortex was apparently responding to particular features such as the lines and bars in the physical environment.

While they rarely articulated this claim, these scientists took for granted that both the search for such features and the formation of fuller images or descriptions were directed by visual knowledge already stored in the brains of higher animals. Seeing, they argued, requires first knowing what one is looking at. They concluded that vision in higher animals uses feature detectors to find vertical, horizontal, and oblique lines among other forms; and that stored in memory cells is preexisting information, with which the responses to the feature detectors have to be compared. Physiology appeared to justify the nineteenth-century view that the brain contains visual memory images, and was beginning to suggest ways in which this information might be used to recognize objects.

On the basis of these findings, scientists in the field of artificial intelligence decided it should be easy to build seeing machines that could identify and manipulate objects by matching electronically registered shapes with images stored in the computers' memory. This, however, proved considerably more difficult than had been anticipated, in part because much of what we see has nothing to do with the shapes and locations of physical objects—for example, shadows, variations in illumination, dust, or different textures. Which features are important for seeing an object, and which can be ignored? In addition, the computer scientists found that a seeing robot would need an enormous memory stuffed with photos, drawings, and three-dimensional reproductions of grandmas, teddy bears, bugs, and whatever else the robot might encounter in its preassigned tasks. They tried to simplify the problem by restricting visual scenes to minute worlds of toy blocks and office desks; and concentrated on writing programs that could effectively and rapidly search computer memories for images that matched those in the robot's eye.

David Marr: Beyond Artificial Intelligence

While some of these programs worked very well, neither they nor the neurophysiological studies had, by the 1970s, added anything new to the old and by now well-accepted view that each function is localized in the brain. Then, between 1970 and 1980, David Marr reformulated the fundamental questions that studies of brain function must answer.

Marr thought that the very limitations of the artificial-intelligence approach meant that some fundamental issues were being overlooked, both by the physiologists and by the computer scientists. By confining their worlds to toy blocks and office desks, the artificial-intelligence scientists had failed to confront such basic questions as what constitutes an object (the horse? the rider? or horse *and* rider?) and how it can be separated from the rest of a visual image. Marr noted that the parts of a visual image that we name—those that have a meaning for us—do not necessarily have visually distinctive characteristics that can be uniquely specified in a computer program. The same circle could represent the sun or a wheel or a tabletop, depending on the scene.

This is reminiscent of the various ways in which the brain may categorize a particular set of articulatory movements of the vocal tract as one phoneme or another, depending on context. So, too, the visual scene may be broken down in many different ways, and the significance of a circle or a square will vary depending on the rest of the scene. Artificial-intelligence researchers mistakenly assumed that the squares, circles, telephones, and desks that make up one visual scene must have the same significance in every other visual scene in which they appear; and that they therefore could be stored in computer memories for comparison with visual stimuli. It was as though the computer scientists were trying to simulate Dejerine's idea of visual memory centers (see part 1); and ultimately, as Marr noted, they failed. There was something wrong with the whole approach.

Marr was led to these insights, shortly after his arrival at MIT in 1973 at the age of twenty-eight, when he heard the English psychologist Elizabeth Warrington speak about patients with damage to the right side of the brain who had no trouble identifying water buckets and similar objects seen from the side, yet were unable to identify them from above; while another group of patients with damage to the brain's left side readily identified the water bucket from both angles (see figure 3.1).

Warrington's talk suggested to Marr that the brain stores information about the use and function of objects separately from information about their shape, and that our visual system permits us to recognize objects even

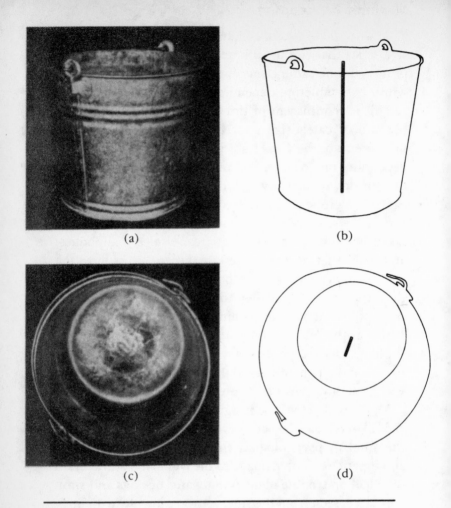

(a)

(b)

(c)

(d)

Figure 3.1.

Two views of a water bucket from the side (a) and top (c). In (c) the principal
axis of symmetry is foreshortened (d), and recognizing the object as a bucket
is therefore more difficult.

SOURCE: D. Marr and H. K. Nishihara, "Representation and Recognition of the Spatial
Organization of Three-Dimensional Shapes," *Proceedings of the Royal Society of London B200.*

though we cannot name them or describe their function.* In part, Marr's view was perfectly consistent with localizationist orthodoxy: different parts of the brain serve different functions, and the relevant memory images are stored in each functional unit. But when he suggested that we can recognize shapes without any stored images he was hardly presenting the orthodox view.

The Goals of the Visual System

Marr began by asking what the visual system does. The frog's, for example, identifies flies that make good meals—and tasty flies are, for a frog's brain, always moving. The visual system of a fly, on the other hand, needs to locate surfaces on which the fly can land. If a surface suddenly increases in size, or "explodes," the fly's brain will assume that an appropriate surface is nearby and will cut its wing power and extend its legs in preparation for landing. Since higher animals spend much of their time moving around and gathering food, one of the major tasks of their visual systems is to identify and describe three-dimensional shapes so that they can be avoided without much fuss or picked up and examined with relative ease. One of the goals of a frog's visual system, then, is to locate moving specks in the two-dimensional retinal image; while the fly's visual system will want to know when there is a surface large enough to land on; and higher animals use the two-dimensional retinal image to derive descriptions of three-dimensional objects.† Failure to identify the goal of a visual system can lead to misinterpretation of physiological data.

*Warrington was describing work she had done with A. M. Taylor.
†Tomaso Poggio, now at MIT, arrived at a similar formulation at about the same time and was one of Marr's closest collaborators.

By formulating the problem in terms of goals, Marr was emphasizing the adaptive nature of behavior. Human beings and other animals must be capable of manipulating their environments in ways that will permit their survival. Yet since the nature of a particular environment is unpredictable, the idea of goals suggests what an animal must be able to do in any environment. It suggests the limits of the ways in which stimuli may be interpreted, and at the same time emphasizes that, given those limits, stimuli must be "interpreted" in a broad way. Stimuli must be analyzed, then, not in terms of fixed memories but rather in ways that will make it possible for the animal to determine whether the stimuli may be important in one way or another.

Given, for example, that mobile animals must be able to recognize shapes in order to avoid obstacles or to manipulate objects, it is an important goal of the visual system to derive shape from visual stimuli. However, the ways in which shapes are important for an animal may be quite different for a snake, whose mobility is confined to serpentine, crawling movements on the ground, and for a four-legged dog. A dog may jump for a bone hanging from a branch of a tree, whereas the snake will have to crawl up the trunk of the tree; therefore, the visual stimuli will be used to facilitate jumping in the case of the dog and crawling in the case of the snake. A "goal" of the visual system might be the identification of shape, but there is no absolute notion of shape, since what is important about shape will be different for the individual animal, given its physical capabilities, its past experiences, and present circumstances. Implicit, therefore, in the idea of goals—though Marr did not pursue this line of thought—is that seeing shapes may be accomplished independently of any memory system; and that stimuli are not fixed pieces of information coming from the environment, but rather information must be formed out of the stimuli in terms of individual needs and desires. Goals determine the kinds of information—in a very broad sense—that the brain is capable of deriving from environmental clues.

Only after we have understood the goals of a visual system—what Marr called "level one" of understanding—can we study the procedures (or programs) that visual system uses to achieve its goals, Marr's second level. For example, given the fact that we see a visual border between two regions that are distinguished by different densities of dots, what procedure does the brain follow in order to establish this border? How is the brain *programmed* to identify the border? Does it use a procedure that involves measuring the distances between dots and noting where these distances change, or one that involves counting the number of dots in an area of a fixed size and noting where the number of dots changes?

Or do procedures differ from one brain to another, and even within the same brain depending on the circumstances? Marr believed that the brain is specifically programmed for the performance of such tasks and that such programs could be considered a form of inherited memory. There is no need, however, for a program that could match images that fall on the retina with images stored in a memory. On the contrary, Marr was suggesting that programs conceived in accordance with principles to be outlined could derive visual shapes from retinal images in which the visual characteristics of a scene—especially the shapes that make it up—are not evident. Shapes could be derived from a retinal image without any prior knowledge of them (as required by traditional artificial intelligence, as well as by traditional nineteenth- and twentieth-century neurological approaches), using a limited number of programs (procedures) that operate on visual stimuli in the retina. The programs, of course, were carefully *designed*, rather than learned, suggesting that Marr had not fully solved the problem. For it seems unlikely, from a biological point of view, that such programs could be inherited. Nonetheless, the demonstration that a procedure (program) functioning independently of any memory system could recognize shapes gives us powerful reason to suspect that there are biological solutions to the problem of memory which are not dependent on any fixed memory store either, as will be discussed in part 4. Marr's work, therefore, suggested that there was a way out of the numerous problems created by the notion of a fixed memory, above all, the problem evident in a careful examination of the clinical evidence that the idea of fixed memories fails to account for the importance of context in *all* forms of recognition. Marr did not fully develop these ideas, and therefore his work reflects a mixture of contemporary ideas about functional specialization with a radical approach to memory. Indeed, Marr often used his work to justify arguments for functional specialization, overlooking its radical implications.

The Computing Brain and Modularity

The second fundamental idea in Marr's approach is the modern descendant of localizationism: the concept that the visual (or any brain) function can be broken down into individual capacities, or *modules*. Our seeing a tree as a three-dimensional object does not depend on our first recognizing it as a tree. Indeed, we can see things as three-dimensional without knowing what they are; and Marr argued that vision generally consists of many more or less independent subtasks (recognizing trees, seeing in three dimensions), which can be studied independently. This is his principle of modular design: tree recognition and three-dimensional viewing are independent modules. It is not surprising that our brains accomplish tasks, such as seeing and hearing, by solving many independent problems that make up the general task. Otherwise, new capacities that appeared in the course of evolution would have had to develop in perfect form all at once. In Marr's words, modular design is

important because if a process is not designed in this way, a small change in one place has consequences in many other places. As a result, the process as a whole is extremely difficult to debug or to improve, whether by a human designer or in the course of natural evolution, because a small change to improve one part has to be accomplished by many simultaneous, compensatory changes elsewhere. The principle of modular design does not forbid weak interactions between different modules in a task.[1]

Whether the entire brain is made up of the separate functional units Marr called modules is ultimately an empirical question. It could be that new capacities emerge in ways quite unrelated to the idea of modular design, as will be argued in part 4. Nonetheless, brain modularity has become an influential concept, and Marr's work has provided one of the more compelling arguments in its favor to date.

One of the visual system's modules according to this view was spectacularly demonstrated by Bela Julesz in 1960. Using a computer, he created two identical copies of a random collection of black dots on a white background, so that no meaningful image was discernible. On one copy he displaced a square area of dots, filling in the empty space created by the displacement with more random dots. Still neither copy revealed any pattern to the unaided eye. (See figure 3.2.) When viewed in a stereoscope, however—the left eye seeing one display and the right eye the other—the two displays are fused into one, and a square jumps out at the viewer and appears to be floating above a surface of random dots. From the two-dimensional surface, the brain involuntarily derives a three-dimensional image.

The displays were prepared in this manner in order to test how much information is necessary for seeing a three-dimensional image. The only difference between the two patterns is the offset square area, which can be revealed only by comparing the two displays in a stereoscope. The fact that when the patterns are stereoscopically fused the displaced area appears to float tells us that the sensation of three dimensions is created with only one piece of information—that the square has been displaced in one of the patterns. Since, apart from the square area, all the points in the two images coincide, the brain calculates that the dots in the square area are at a different depth from the rest of the display. Of course, this does not happen immediately, and on repetition one *knows* one wants to see a 3-D image.

This important process, called *stereopsis,* is, for Marr, a module. Presented with different measures of displacement of some sets of points as opposed to other sets, the brain compulsively derives different depths within an image. Though we *know* the floating square does not exist, we will always see it. Without any distinctive visual cues (the individual displays are collections of random dots), the brain is able to establish an accurate correspondence between the dots at the same locations in the two images. It does not confuse the dots that make up the

(a)

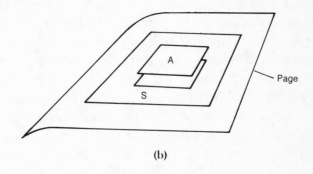

(b)

Figure 3.2.

Random-dot stereograms. Each of the patterns (a) is a random collection of
dots—neither one contains any regular shapes. The patterns are not identical,
however: in one of them a square of dots has been displaced. When viewed
through a stereoscope, the dot patterns fuse into a single image in which a
square can be seen floating in space (b).

SOURCE: John P. Frisby, *Seeing* (Oxford: Oxford University Press, 1980), p. 79.

displaced square with those in the background. To do this, Marr argues, the brain uses certain assumptions, rules, and processes that have been called *computations*.

The computational approach to the brain contains elements of a radically new view of memory but within a framework that is still profoundly "localizationist." Thus, on the one hand, it describes procedures (computations) that can, for example, within a given visual scene, group visual stimuli in certain coherent ways, such that shapes are separated out of the two-dimensional retinal image, without any reliance on a fixed memory. However, the recognition of a shape as a "cube," that is, the *naming* of the shape, still relies on access to a fixed memory. In fact, the kinds of images that can be derived from visual, or other, stimuli are limited by the particular preprogrammed computational procedures. Yet recognition, naming, depends on the *actual* context in which the thing seen or heard happens to be. Dejerine's patient Oscar failed to recognize letters and multidigit numbers because he could not relate the letters and numbers he was looking at to one another. Shapes, with which Marr is principally concerned, are seen differently in different visual settings. The sense of a stimulus depends not only on past experiences, which are important in helping determine what procedure or procedures may be appropriate, but on the present context as well. The computational approach assumes that the kinds of procedures that might be appropriate for a given task or set of tasks (seeing in three dimensions, for example) are relatively fixed and that, therefore, new ways of organizing environmental stimuli (ultimately, new ways of "understanding" the world) are a consequence of applying the same procedures to an ever-increasing mass of information that has been stored in an individual's brain over time.

Machine Recognition

That the brain might be able to create an entirely new procedure, and that newer "understandings," newer *Gestalts*, might be a consequence of such new creations, is a possibility that has not been properly considered. If the brain can create new procedures, then we have a much broader way of explaining its generalizing capacities. And then, of course, the issue is no longer what specific procedures are available for a given task, but how the brain's procedures are created, how they are developed over time, and why a particular set of procedures might be used at a given moment. In fact, the brain's extraordinary role in altering the environment to which it must adapt becomes more readily explained if it can be shown to create new ways (procedures) of organizing stimuli. The computational approach—modularity—implies that the brain has relatively fixed goals and therefore it fails to explain our ability to adapt to drastically different environments, be they those of the cave dweller of 30,000 years ago, or those of the world of the computer. Modularity, like the earlier doctrine of localization, implies that the ways in which we can understand the world—the possible categories of knowledge—are relatively fixed. And yet, as the historical record shows, we not only create new environments but our ways of understanding any given scene or event, at a particular time, are very different from person to person.

If we all viewed the world in identical terms, there would have been no history, no change, or, in the well-known passage of Thomas Hobbes, "no knowledge of the face of the earth; no account of time; no arts; no letters; no society."[2] It is human diversity, not just common goals, that has given rise to culture. This, not the localization of function, is the real lesson of the nineteenth-century studies of brain-damaged patients. For those patients often demonstrated linguistic handicaps that are probably better explained as a loss of higher powers of generalization (with consequent limitations on their abilities to organize words and sentences), rather than as the loss of a specific linguistic function. And because linguistic signs (letters, words, numbers, and so on) can help create these generalizations, their sense will change in varying circumstances, suggesting that there are no fixed symbols anywhere in the brain. Perhaps in its failure to free itself from fixed symbols, the computational approach ultimately stifles what could have been a new view of memory as procedure. For all computations, whether they be in adding machines or computers, require some kind of symbols ("representations").* In 1976 David Marr suggested that the visual system of the brain computes a symbol that he called the *primal sketch*.

Symbols in the Brain: The Primal Sketch

Our retinas consist of some 160 million light receptors which are sensitive to varying levels of illumination, ranging from black to white; these are usually called *gray*

---

*Different symbolic representations make explicit and usable different pieces of information. Various symbolic systems, for example, have been created to represent numbers throughout history. Arabic numbers (1, 2, 3, 4, and so on) make explicit the powers of 10 (10^0, 10^1, 10^2, and so on) that go into the composition of that number: 19 is 9×10^0 plus 1×10^1. Binary numbers make explicit the powers of 2 that compose a given number (2^0, 2^1, 2^2, and so on): 10011 is 19 in the binary system. Marr claimed that the extreme resistance of Roman numerals to being manipulated (multiply XX by XXI, for example, rather than 20 by 21) explains why the Romans never made any significant contributions to mathematics.

The symbolism, however, does not affect the goals of a computation, unless it makes the required information impossible to retrieve. We can add with both Roman numerals and Arabic numbers. The goal (Marr's first level of understanding) will be the same but the procedures will not (Marr's second level of understanding). And we can implement these procedures with an old-fashioned adding machine or a pocket calculator (Marr's third level of understanding). The machinery we use will not affect the nature of the computation, be it multiplication or addition.

levels. The image cast upon the retina is therefore broken up into a two-dimensional arrangement consisting of the different levels of light intensity reaching the receptors, an arrangement similar to the dot patterns on a television screen. From this pattern the brain creates the three-dimensional scenes that we actually see, and in which we are able to distinguish objects, describe their shapes, locations, colors, textures, and so on. Since we all agree on the general makeup of a given scene, we can say, according to Marr, that our brains compute roughly the same unique symbolic representations from the gray-level images.

Marr argued that in the first stages of visual processing the brain computes a two-dimensional sketch, which he called the *primal sketch,* from the gray-level retinal image. We are not conscious of this computation, but the symbol that is derived from the retinal image is quite familiar to us. It looks very much like a rough drawing. (This is the reason, he believed, we can make sense of artists' sketches; they are similar to the symbols computed in our brains.)

But how does the brain compute this image? Many of the dots that make up the gray-level retinal image are identically "gray," that is, they show the same level of illumination. The brain derives the primal sketch by noting where the level of grayness changes from one set of dots to another set. The lines that make up the primal sketch represent the extent, the magnitude (the thickness of the line), and the direction of the changes. (See figure 3.3.)

A black wall, for example, will create a set of identical responses in the receptors in the eye; but if there is a white square in the middle of the wall, along the borders of the square there will be a change in the amount of

(a)

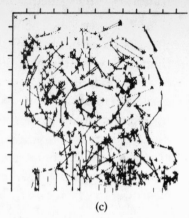

(c)

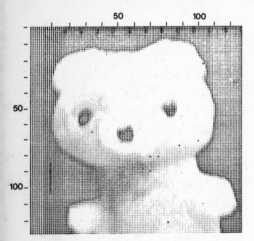

Figure 3.3.

A computer simulation of the gray-level pattern (b) produced when viewing a teddy bear (a), along with the primal sketch (c) that the visual system constructs so as to make the pattern perceptible. Each dot in the image is the equivalent of a retinal cell measuring light intensity at that point in the image. (The human eye has many more receptor cells than in this simulation.) From the gray-level image the brain derives *all* the visual information about shapes, surface contours, and so on. It makes explicit information that is only implicit in the gray-level image.

To do so, the brain integrates the pattern of dots into a simplified image that indicates the extent, magnitude, and directions of the intensity changes—Marr's primal sketch. When we view a gray-level image, such as the one shown here, our brain processes it much as it does the retinal image. That is why we see the teddy bear in (b). If the image were not processed by extracting a primal sketch from it, we would see just a collection of dots of varying intensities. SOURCE: John P. Frisby, *Seeing* (Oxford: Oxford University Press, 1980), p. 110.

light being reflected. This fact will be recorded in the primal sketch as a line indicating the extent and orientation of the change—in other words, as a sketch of a square. For the purposes of the primal sketch, the computational approach suggests that the brain ignores the uniform areas of whiteness within the square or blackness outside it. Therefore, what is visually significant occurs where the illumination changes. And the same is true of three-dimensional objects. It is along the edges of an object, or where there are variations in the smoothness of a surface, that the intensity of reflected light changes. A flat, uniformly lighted surface will give a uniform gray-level retinal image.

The brain computes the changes in the gray-level image because they mark the physically or visually significant areas of a scene. In making this computation, the brain uses no previously acquired knowledge, its neuronal machinery having evolved in such a way as to allow it to make these computations automatically. The brain, in computing a primal sketch, is trying to analyze the physical or visually significant characteristics of the environment. Marr drew the conclusion that implicit in the brain's analysis (or computations) is the assumption that edges, changes in contours, and so on are where light intensities change in the retinal image. This assumption, of course, is written nowhere in the brain but is presupposed by its design. Once we recognize it, we can understand what the brain is doing.

Such implicit assumptions are in Marr's view as essential to our understanding of brain function as to our understanding of any mechanical or electrical device. If our assumptions are sufficiently general, they will explain why a particular task or set of tasks must be carried out by the brain or mechanical device and why no other task will satisfy those assumptions. The cash register in the supermarket is an example of a device that performs a specific task—addition. But why is it constructed to perform addition rather than square roots? Because the implicit assumptions in our notions of fairness in the exchange of money and goods can be satisfied only through the use of addition. Those assumptions are: (1) buying nothing should cost nothing; (2) the order in which the items are presented for purchase should not affect the total amount paid; (3) dividing the items into piles and paying for each pile separately should not affect the total amount paid; (4) if an item is bought and then returned, the total cost should be zero.

These assumptions, which make up our notion of fairness in the supermarket, happen to be the mathematical conditions that define addition. No other kind of computation will satisfy all of these assumptions all of the time. Of course, the assumptions are nowhere to be found in the cash register. They are implied by the fact that cash registers were *designed* to add prices.

The assumptions about the physical environment that are implied by the computations the brain performs on gray-level images are implicit in the same way. Since the brain always performs the same kinds of computations on the gray-level images, there must be certain general assumptions to explain why the brain performs those computations and not others. As we have seen, the brain's calculations of intensity changes in the gray-level image are based on the assumption that changes in light intensities can represent physically or visually significant parts of the environment.

Marr called the implicit assumptions "constraints." Without the notion of constraints, he argued, we would not be able to talk about, or to understand, brain function. The constraint I have mentioned—that changes in light intensity can represent a physical edge—requires a further refinement if the brain is not to make many mistakes about the environment. Marr was able to make this refinement by reexamining a neurophysiological mechanism that had been the subject of considerable discussion since its discovery in the late 1960s. Physiologists then found that some cells in the brain are sensitive to lines that are widely separated, while other cells respond to finer details. They concluded that there are several networks, or channels, of neurons, each sensitive to different spatial frequencies. The channels sensitive to coarse frequencies "see" only intensity changes that are widely separated, whereas the finer channels can distinguish those that are closer together. Therefore, Marr argued, intensity changes found in the large channels that coincide with those in the smaller channels represent, for the visual system, physical changes in the image, such as an edge or a change of contour. Whenever what is found in the large channels cannot be accounted for by the information in the smaller channels, the brain makes the implicit assumption that the information in the two channels has different physical causes.

In the cubist image reproduced in figure 3.4, for example, we can see Charlie Chaplin only by screwing up our eyes because no information about spatial frequencies is being provided for the middle channels sensitive to details that are neither coarse nor fine. The brain therefore assumes that the information in the large channels is not related to that in the finer channels. If it were, there would be some overlap with the information in the middle channels, but no information is coming from the middle frequency range. When we screw up our eyes, the finer channels are eliminated and we see only Charlie

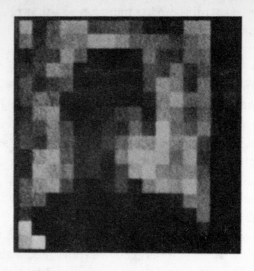

Figure 3.4.

A cubist image constructed so that Charlie Chaplin becomes visible only when the viewer squints.

SOURCE: John P. Frisby, *Seeing* (Oxford: Oxford University Press, 1980), p. 120.

Chaplin in the larger channels. The brain is no longer confused by information for which it cannot account. This suggests, in Marr's view, how seriously the brain takes physical constraints in the visual system: they are apparently implicit in the neuronal machinery of the brain, just as the rules of addition are implicit in the mechanism of the cash register.

But are they? After all, there are many ways of viewing the cubist image. Whether the brain categorizes different sets of stimuli (broad versus narrow channel) as related or unrelated clearly depends on a variety of circumstances. For sure, recognizing Charlie Chaplin, and the associations one might have with his image, depends on experience. The image one sees without squinting is as real as the one seen when one does squint. Is the brain being cheated out of seeing Charlie Chaplin should one not bother to squint?

The example suggests that the search for a physically coherent image (the use of physical constraints) is but one of many ways in which the brain categorizes visual stimuli. And the computational approach, requiring built-in assumptions and procedures that derive specific *kinds* of images, fails to account for the variety of ways in which we categorize our perceptions. And it fails to account for how experience affects perception. Adding new programs will not solve the problem. Since there are an enormous number of ways to categorize a scene, it will be impossible to predict what programs will be appropriate for a given individual's experiences. That the physical attributes of the world are a critical factor in our visual impressions is a consequence not of any programs in the brain, but of our experience in the world. How experience alters our brains and thus influences the ways in which we categorize will be discussed in part 4. For the moment, it is important to note that computations cannot explain the effect of experience on our perceptions. Learning is, even in Marr's theory, stored in fixed images derived through computation. Perception is considered independent of experience. However, experience does alter perception. What we see in a painting, for example, is deeply affected by our cultural background.

What is wrong with the computational approach is that the procedures that are postulated as the basis of perception fail to incorporate experience in a way that would make them truly procedures of recognition and memory. Perception, recognition, memory are not separate processes, as the computational view implies, but an integral procedure. In separating learning from perception, Marr's theory gives the barest outlines of a procedural approach to memory. The use of fixed memory images ignores the importance of present context (a reference to the actual scene in making identification, not a reference to a stored image); and the failure to incorporate experience and learning in perception means relying on fixed procedures for perceiving images, and therefore ignores the role of learning in perception. There are no symbols in the brain; there are patterns of activity that acquire different meanings in different contexts. Marr was making too many concessions to the localizationist tradition.

Nonetheless, he did show how a procedure could derive a three-dimensional image from the two-dimensional retinal image. That this can be accomplished without matching sensory images to fixed memory images is a major blow to the very localizationist tradition to which Marr paid such homage. And what is more important, it suggests that procedures might be the key to an understanding of recognition and memory. Unfortunately, Marr's notion of procedure as a fixed program was too limited; but the procedures he described are worth examining as an example of how recognition of shape can be accomplished without a fixed memory.

The 2½-D Sketch

From the flat primal sketch, the brain derives, according to Marr's theory, the next major symbol, or representation, which he called the "2½-D sketch." This makes it explicit that an object has three dimensions but only from the viewer's perspective, without providing information about the object's appearance from other perspectives. The brain uses a number of independent calculations (modules) to help it form this new symbol, automatically analyzing the separate effects of shading and motion, to mention only two of the factors it takes into account.

To show that the brain can derive the structure of an object from seeing it in motion, Marr's colleague Shimon Ullman painted random dots on two transparent cylinders of different diameters and then placed one within the other (see figure 3.5). Light was projected through the cylinders onto a screen, so that random dots were visible on the screen but not on the outlines of the cylinders. When the cylinders are stationary, we see only the ran-

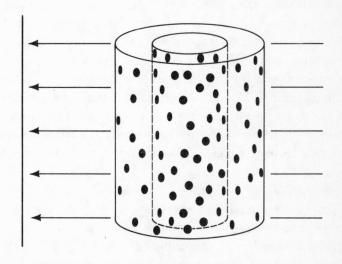

Figure 3.5.

Ullman's rotating cylinders. Dots painted on the cylinders are projected onto the screen. When the cylinders are not rotating, a random collection of dots is seen. The outlines of the cylinders are clearly visible, however, when they rotate in opposite directions.

SOURCE: Shimon Ullman, *The Interpretation of Visual Motion* (Cambridge: MIT Press, 1979), p. 135.

dom dots. But when the cylinders are rotated in opposite directions, the two rotating cylinders are clearly visible on the screen. Ullman was able to show that if the brain assumes that an object is rigid, then it can derive its structure when it is moving. Without the'implied assumption or constraint of rigidity, as when viewing the surface of a stream, no clear structure can be discerned.

Numerous experiments have claimed to show that rigidity is assumed in the visual system and plays an important part in our perception of objects. For example, if a square is projected onto a screen and then its sides are alternately expanded and contracted, one would expect to see first a small square, then a large square, then a small square, and so on. In fact, one will see a square that does not change in size, but that recedes from the viewer, approaches the viewer, and so on. The visual system misinterprets the cues as if one were observing a rigid object. But, again, does this mean that rigidity is "programmed" in the brain rather than learned? We have all seen rigid objects such as a wavy plastic surface, and recognized that they are rigid imitations of the "structureless" surface of water.

The 3-D Model

The 2½-D sketch tells the brain about an object or a person only from the viewer's perspective; it does not give one a full sense of an object in space. How can the brain compute a generalized view of an object—what Marr called the "3-D model"—from the 2½-D sketch so that one can be aware of its full structure and its situation in space? According to work Marr did with H. K. Nishihara, the brain will try to determine whether any line can, when drawn through the 2½-D sketch, establish what he calls its "basic pattern of symmetry." There is a basic symmetry between a human being's right and left sides, and we can imagine a line running through the middle of the head and torso establishing that symmetry. Not all objects have such symmetry, but most do; and Marr and Nishihara's theory applies only to these.

It might be difficult for the brain to derive the principal line of symmetry from the 2½-D sketch when it is very much foreshortened at the angle from which an object is observed—for example, when a water bucket is viewed from the top rather than the side (see figure 3.1). Human beings and animals have one principal line of symmetry running through the head and the body and many other branching lines of symmetry running through the arms, legs, fingers, toes, and so on (see figure 3.6). Stick figures of animals constructed out of pipe cleaners make explicit these basic lines of symmetry, and Marr and Nishihara suggested that they make sense to us because they resemble the lines that the brain in fact computes. The brain goes on to provide a full image identifiable from any point of view by, according to this theory, automatically transposing the contours it has derived from the 2½-D sketch onto axes of symmetry, giving us the three-dimensional image we see: Marr's 3-D model.

The importance of symmetry in visual computations is shown by two psychological consequences that follow from it. Psychologists have demonstrated that we see objects as collections of individual parts, and the 3-D model not only explains why (because different lines of symmetry make up the symbol) but tells how we tend to decompose the objects we look at (we do so by tracing the principal lines of symmetry to their branches). This also tells us something about our ability to generalize ("Joan and Jane are women") and yet to describe distinguishing

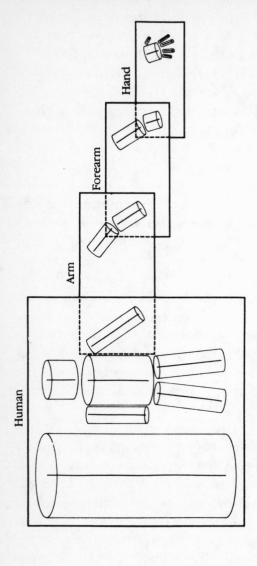

Figure 3.6.

The axes of symmetry that the brain may derive in analyzing a human figure, according to Marr.

SOURCE: D. Marr and H. K. Nishihara, "Representation and Recognition of the Spatial Organization of Three-Dimensional Shapes," *Proceedings of the Royal Society of London B200.*

characteristics ("Joan is the blonde; Jane, the brunette"). The principal lines of symmetry give general descriptions, while the finer distinguishing details are drawn from an analysis of the branching lines of symmetry.

The importance of the principal lines of symmetry in understanding visual material is perhaps best illustrated by recalling the story of Elizabeth Warrington's patients (see page 117). Those who had difficulty recognizing water buckets were viewing them from a perspective that foreshortened their principal line of symmetry. In Marr's theory this line is so important for recognition that, when it is foreshortened, some brain-damaged patients have difficulty identifying the object (see figure 3.6).

Such, in any event, is Marr's explanation of these studies. The reasons why we can make sense of photographs from different views, or why brain-damaged patients cannot make sense of them, may be quite different for each individual. We each analyze visual scenes in different ways. Warrington failed to study how varying contexts would have affected the perceptions of her patients. The use of symmetry, as Marr suggested, to derive shape may or may not be an important procedure for many individuals. But what is striking is that procedures, not the loss of memory, can explain the clinical problems.

Marr did not realize that such procedures, if related back to the original scene, would constitute recognition; and that in this way perception, experience (which affects the procedures used), and context are linked into a "memory." Rather, in part because he thought that procedures were fixed and therefore not affected by experience, and in part because he believed that procedures therefore extracted specific pieces of information from a visual scene that are perceived by *everyone*, he argued that recognition ultimately depends on a match with acquired knowledge.

Naming the Object

Indeed, having found a way to show that a computer derives shape without any acquired knowledge, Marr nonetheless resorted to the concept of a memory store for the naming of objects. We can name and recognize a 3-D model as a tree or a bucket, he concluded, because it can be matched with acquired knowledge that is stored and catalogued in our brains. But the search for catalogued information—a problem that had preoccupied the artificial-intelligence community when it first tried to build seeing machines—occurs only at this final stage of visual processing. Few had imagined that so much information about shapes could be extracted from the retinal images *before* catalogued information had to be tapped.

Just how much we can "see" without drawing on acquired knowledge was suggested by Warrington's second group of patients, who had no trouble discerning the shapes of objects from unusual viewpoints but were unable to name them or to describe their function. But this reflects a rather common experience. How often have we walked into a hardware store, for example, and *seen* objects, but had no idea of their use or function?

It is the idea of catalogued information that is a mistake, however. It fails to relate the derived image to the environmental sources of that image and hence to its context; and it fails to take account of the fact that naming, too, is context-sensitive. It is the inability to establish contexts, not the loss of any memory images or words, that is the reason patients have difficulties naming things. (See, for example, Low's case, pages 87–88.)

Though Marr found evidence for the symbolic representations he had proposed in some works of art, what is perhaps more striking is how these works reflect the very different perceptions of the world of each artist:

It is interesting to think about which representations the different artists concentrate on and sometimes disrupt. The pointillists, for example, are tampering primarily with the [gray-level] image; the rest of the scheme is left intact, and the picture has a conventional appearance otherwise. Picasso, on the other hand, clearly disrupts most at the 3-D model level. The three-dimensionality of his figures is not realistic. An example of someone who creates primarily at the surface representation stage [2½-D sketch] is a little harder—Cezanne perhaps?[3]

It is not different representations but different procedures that incorporate our varied experiences, that the varieties of art reflect. And integral to our visual experiences are our explorations of the world around us through movements. Indeed, it appears that we are *not* born with fixed rules for deriving shapes in a visual scene. Infants do *not* perceive connected objects, of uniform color and simple and regular shape. They do, however, see partly hidden objects (for example, when the middle of the object is occluded) even though the exposed surfaces may not be of the same color. Uniform movement appears to be critical to an infant's ability to classify an object as an object. Therefore objects are not categorized by the visual system alone; movements appear to be a necessary concomitant. As Kellman and Spelke note:

The conception of objects that we would attribute to infants would appear to be the central conception of objects that humans hold as adults. When adults encounter some body of matter, we tend to consider it an object if it is coherent and moveable, even if it is highly irregular in shape and substance. We would be far less likely to consider such matter an object, however, if it consisted of several separate and separately moveable bodies. Uniformity of shape and substance are characteristic, but not essential, properties of objects. Coherence over movement may be an essential property, at the center of our conception of the world.

If this view is correct, then knowledge of material objects may be one domain of cognition, perhaps one of many, in which our knowledge is elaborated with development, but is never fundamentally reorganized. A child who first conceives of the world as composed of coherent and moveable things will tend to focus on such things to perceive and to learn about. It is perhaps through learning that children come to know that coherent, moveable things tend to be regular in shape and color and that certain of these things belong to certain kinds, like cats and telephones. But objects—unitary, persisting, moveable things—are what children will learn about. Our original conceptions thus will tend to perpetuate themselves in everything we learn, and will remain our deepest conceptions of the world.[4]

The computational view, which opens up radical new possibilities to our understanding of memory and recognition, takes into account neither such developmental changes nor the ways in which our individual histories, the contexts in which we act, can affect *what* we see at a particular moment. Dejerine's patient could not read music because he was unable to organize the notes or to establish a context in which they made sense. Marr's primal sketch is independent of context. Rules, computational procedures for deriving shapes, are too rigid. We can certainly see without knowing what we are looking at. But *knowing* alters what and how we see. Knowing the function of a pair of pliers will profoundly alter the way we see the pliers. And even "not knowing" what we are looking at occurs in a context of accumulated knowledge and experience that inevitably affects how we see whatever we happen to be looking at. Fixed memory stores, we have already seen, cannot accommodate the factors of context and history. Computations—the use of procedures in a limited way—bring us closer to a better solution but still fail to explain a crucial aspect of our perceptual capabilities: how our past affects our present view of the world, and how our coordinated movements, our past and present explorations of the world, influence our perceptions.

Another Machine—PDP: Hidden Memories

If Marr's computations are too rigid to account for history and context, another recent development in machine intelligence claims to have solved the problem using a device known as a *parallel distributed processor* (PDP). This machine, basically a pattern associator, consists of networks of interconnected nodes that can be in an "on" or "off" state.

PDP machines are input-output devices (see figure 3.7). Input nodes are activated to encode a particular piece of information (such as "tulips"), and output nodes are activated to encode a related piece of information (such as "red"). The machine "learns" the relation between tulips and red, by adjusting the connecting weights (the resistances between the nodes that make up the network between the input and the output), so that whenever "tulips" is encoded in the input, the code for "red" will appear in the output. The machine can also "learn" other

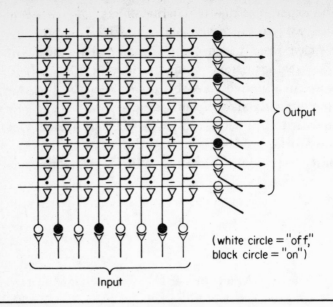

(white circle = "off,"
black circle = "on")

Output

Input

Figure 3.7.

A PDP network. When a given input code and the desired output code are put into the machine at the respective "input" and "output" terminals, the "weightings" of the intervening nodes in the network are altered so that future inputs of the given code will always produce the desired output. As new input-output relations are added to the machine, the network weightings readjust so that previously learned relations can still be produced on the machine. (The weightings within the network represent a *summation* of all learned input-output patterns.)

SOURCE: David E. Rumelhart, James L. McClelland, and the PDP Research Group, *Parallel Distributed Processing: Explorations in the Microstructure of Cognition*, vol. 2, *Psychological and Biological Models* (Cambridge: MIT Press, 1986), p. 227.

associations without losing previously acquired relations. Thus the weightings in the network adjust in such a way that, given the code for tulip, the code for red will appear in the output, and, given the code for daffodils, the code for yellow (a subsequently learned pattern) will appear in the output.

Rather than having a particular node represent a specific piece of information, as is common in more conventional computer simulations (strictly localizationist models of the brain), PDP devices use a *group* of nodes to represent a particular piece of information. The connections between the nodes have variable weightings (or resistances), and, by varying the strengths of the connection between nodes, one can alter the information being represented in the network. Therefore the memories are distributed; they have a structure: "What PDP models do is describe the internal structure of the larger units, just as subatomic physics describes the internal structure of the atoms that form the constituents of larger units of chemical structure."[5] Since the information being represented is determined by the pattern of connections of the active nodes, the same individual nodes may be used to represent different items of memory. Superficially, this suggests that there is no fixed memory in a PDP machine. But every item is represented by a specific pattern of activity: an interconnected group of nodes rather than an individual node. Many different patterns of activity can be stored in the same network and some of these patterns will inevitably overlap, suggesting that there are resemblances among stored items and that, therefore, they are in some sense related.

Thus when many items are learned by a PDP machine, the connection strengths become adjusted so that any given item will always produce a given output. This is basically a fixed memory. The distributed network permits the storage of a number of associations over the same nodes, but a specific input will (after proper adjustment of the weights) cause a specific activation of the network and a specific output. The connection strengths, then, represent a *summation* of all learned patterns. Because this "sum" is distributed across the network, however, a given item will activate only that part of the network (the subtotal of weightings) that produces the originally associated output. Encoding "tulips" sorts out from the total connection strengths that part which will cause an output of "red." There is nothing mysterious about this process, and the mathematics of it is well known. It is a little like carrying a sack of mixed fruits and vegetables that weighs five pounds, and knowing that if you reduce the weight of its contents to a half-pound you will find an apple, whereas if you reduce its weight to three-quarters of a pound you will find a potato.

One reason PDP devices have attracted considerable attention is their apparent ability to generalize. If, for example, the machine is given the code for a flower it has never "learned," it will nonetheless associate a color with the flower. But this is hardly surprising, since the new flower will be coded by the programmer in a way that is similar to the codes for the flowers already learned. This is prefabricated "generalization." The overlapping patterns of activity that cause the machine to associate a color with an unknown flower are in the programmer's codes, not in the nature of flowers or colors.

PDP networks categorize and generalize in terms of common patterns of activity—"microfeatures"—which form subsets within larger ensembles. Given two pieces of information, for example, "bite" and "sit," the network will notice the element common to both words. Most stimuli, however, are not organized into neat packets of information like words, or language in general. The brain must first organize the stimuli into "meaningful" wholes. And the ability to form new categories depends on more than finding common subfeatures of stimuli and noting their contextual relations; it depends on combining stimuli, which in themselves have no meaning for an organism, in a variety of ways that will help that organism cope with its environment. In fact, one cannot predict how stimuli, or what combinations of them, will be useful—one of the limitations of any programmed machine. PDP networks generalize from samples of information already given.

But neither can one predict what constitutes *information* for an organism. The brain must try as many combinations of incoming stimuli as possible, and then select those combinations that will help the organism relate to its environment. It is in this sense that present context is crucial to determining the significance of a stimulus or a group of stimuli.

In fact, PDP stimulations are really based on the nineteenth-century principles of localization and the matching of stimuli to fixed memory stores. The "generalizations" of these devices are nothing more than overlapping patterns in *predetermined* codes. Real generalization creates *new* categories of information; and from an organism's point of view, such new categorizations are the consequence of unforeseen elements in the environment.

Take, for example, James McClelland and David Rumelhart's simulation of letter recognition. In their model, they were trying to explain a number of well-known psychological results concerning letter recognition. One striking result was that it is easier to recognize letters in pronounceable nonwords than in unpronounceable nonwords. McClelland and Rumelhart's simulation consisted of a three-layered system in which the bottom layer used feature detectors to identify the various strokes and lines that make up a letter in a given position of a word or a nonword. (Of course, this is *not*

the basis of letter recognition, as we know from Dejerine—see pages 51–52.) This information excites units in
the second layer that represent specific letters in specific
positions. The letter units in turn provide input to the
third layer where specific words are represented (see
figure 3.8). There are various excitatory and inhibitory
inputs between the second and third layers as well as
within each layer, which need not concern us here. The
model demonstrates the superior recognition of letters

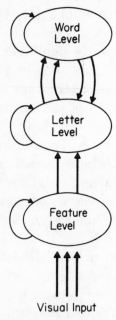

The simplified processing system

Figure 3.8.

The McClelland and Rumelhart system for "reading" pronounceable nonwords and ambiguous letters in words.

SOURCE: J. L. McClelland and D. E. Rumelhart, "An Interactive Activation Model of
Context Effects in Letter Perception: Part 1. An Account of Basic Findings," *Psychological
Review* 88 (1981): 379.

---

in pronounceable nonwords as opposed to non-pronounceable nonwords, because the letters in the pronounceable nonwords activate a "gang" of words in the third level that *nearly fit* the nonword. Since none of the fits is perfect, there is mutual inhibition and excitation both within the word level and between the word and letter levels. Eventually the entire system becomes stable, with many words slightly active. The pronounceable nonword is then represented by a distributed pattern of activity, or so the programmer would interpret the machine's activity. For all the machine has done is to have found *preprogrammed* words that closely resemble the nonword. McClelland and Rumelhart have interpreted this as *explaining* why pronounceable nonwords are more easily recognized. But the explanation is presupposed in the design of the machine!

The same system is capable of deciphering an ambiguous letter, as in figure 3.9. Since the fourth letter of the figure could be either R or K, both letters are excited by the feature detectors. But only the preprogrammed word *WORK* will be excited by the four detectors, since *WORR* will not have been preprogrammed. Inhibitory impulses from the excited *WORK* will block out other possible (preprogrammed) words that could be excited by the three-letter combination *WOR?*. At the same time, excitatory lines will reinforce the final position K, which will have been competing with R at the letter level of the machine. Consequently the K will eventually dominate over the R, and the machine will settle into a state in which the word *WORK* is produced.

But, again, this is simply matching stimuli in ways that have been predetermined; the stimuli have not been classified in a new way, which might be appropriate in this particular case. The partially obscured symbol *must*

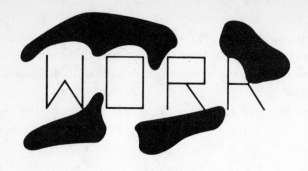

Figure 3.9.

An example of an ambiguous letter. In the McClelland and Rumelhart simulation, the final letter could be read as either an *R* or a *K*. Since the word *WORR* did not exist in the machine's vocabulary, the machine "concluded" that the ambiguous letter was a *K*, making up the word *WORK*. But the word *WORR* could well be an acronym, and some readers might see the final letter as an *A*, or merely as an obscured nonletter—possibilities that show a kind of generalization of which the PDP machines are incapable.

SOURCE: J. L. McClelland and D. E. Rumelhart, "An Interactive Activation Model of Context Effects in Letter Perception: Part I. An Account of Basic Findings," *Psychological Review* 88 (1981): 383.

be, for this machine, either an *R* or a *K*. In fact, it is a partially obscured symbol that, depending on the context, could be an *R*, a *K*, or a *R*. But the PDP device is unable to recognize *R* as a symbol. It cannot really categorize new information. Rather, it produces "best fits" based on prestored information, and therefore is doing exactly what the nineteenth-century localizationists argued was the essence of recognition. And like the nineteenth-century localizationists' argument, the PDP machine fails to show how past experience affects our perceptions in ways that produce the *new and unexpected*; it fails to explain how we create new concepts, new ways of viewing the present, new *kinds* of generalizations and categorizations. The issue is not, as the PDP defenders argue, overlapping patterns of activity, but how patterns of activity acquire a significance in a particular context. Very different patterns of activity may have similar meanings, as N. A. Bernstein noted in the 1930s; circular movements made with the arm in various positions are accomplished with very different patterns of muscular innervation (see figure 3.10). And so, too, similar patterns of activity may have very different meanings in new contexts. Remember how a *3* changes its meaning in the number 33,333 (see page 48).

Finally, much has been made of a PDP simulation of past-tense learning in children. Children acquire the past tense in three stages. In the first stage they use a few verbs that are among those most commonly used in the

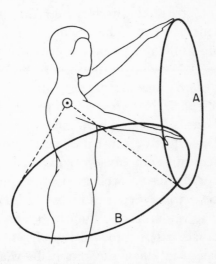

Figure 3.10.

A given figure, such as the circle shown in the illustration, can be drawn using many different combinations of muscular movements.

SOURCE: H. T. A. Whiting, ed., *Human Motor Actions: Bernstein Reassessed* (Amsterdam: Elsevier Science Publishers, North-Holland Publishing Company, 1984), p. 84.

language. Most of these verbs are irregular (for example, *got*, *gave*, *took*, *went*), though there is a small percentage of regular verbs *(needed, looked)*. In the second stage, the child correctly forms the past tense not only of regular verbs but of invented words as well, simply by adding *-ed* to a stem. The child now regularizes the past tense of irregular verbs that he or she had formerly used correctly *(comed,* or *camed)*. Eventually, the previously learned irregular forms reemerge, and the child uses both the regular and irregular forms correctly.

PDP machines that have been given samples of present-tense (input) and past-tense (output) forms of irregular verbs will "learn" these forms and, when given samples of regular present- and past-tense verbs, will tend to regularize the irregular verbs. The machine will eventually adjust and correctly produce both the irregular and regular forms of verbs. The striking parallel between machine and human learning patterns in this case has suggested to some that the brain and the machine are performing similar operations. Yet the machine has been "trained" (given verbs) in a way that parodies the child's learning pattern. As Rumelhart and McClelland admit, "It should be perfectly clear that this training experience exaggerates the difference between early phases of learning and later phases, as well as the abruptness of the transition to a larger corpus of verbs."[6] Children do not hear a few irregular verbs, then many regular verbs. They are in fact exposed to widely different samples of the language. And they use the verbs they learn in sentences.

What is remarkable about the child's use of the past tense is not whether he or she tends to regularize some verbs at certain stages of acquisition, but that the child can distinguish past- and present-tense usage—can establish a context. Furthermore, it is not clear whether the child has acquired a notion of the past tense when he or she uses *come/came*, or (more likely) whether the child hears some sentences in which he or she finds *come* appropriate and others in which *came* seems appropriate, and then applies this acquired knowledge to his or her own productions. At the point where the child begins to regularize irregular past-tense forms, the child probably has a good sense of what past tense means. The tendency to regularize is a generalization about the nature of the past tense, which the child may not have had when a few irregular verbs had been acquired during the early stages of language learning. And it could be that the reemergence of the irregular forms is due to the child's having *relearned* those verbs in the context of his or her new understanding of the past tense.

None of these factors has been considered in the programming of the PDP machines. In fact, the simulation is based on the rather simple assumption that all generalizations are a matching of patterns, whereas powerful generalizations (of which the PDP machines are not capable) are based on establishing completely new and unexpected patterns of relations—such as the *idea* of a past tense! If we are to understand the brain, then we must find processes that make no a priori assumptions about the nature of the world and the nature of stimuli (such as "This is a word," or "This is a noise") and yet permit real generalization from varied samples of stimuli.

Machines versus Biology:
The Problem of Language

Studies of language acquisition in children tend to reinforce the idea that the brain creates its own generalizations about the world. When children learn a language, they do not first learn words and then learn how to organize sentences; they first learn sentences and later come to understand that these are composed of words. "If a child understands an utterance," the English psychologist Margaret Donaldson writes,

it may seem obvious that the words which compose it are "known" and that, in the process of making sense of the utterance, each of these words is given "its meaning." But this is to suppose that a child interprets the language in isolation from its immediate context, which is not what typically happens. . . . Thus a child can begin to learn the meaning of "Do you want some milk?" because when someone picks up a jug and holds it over a cup the intention to offer milk is understood. On this view it is to be expected that for a long time the interpretation of language should remain, for the child, embedded in, and powerfully dependent on, the context of occurrence.[7]

Or, as the American philosopher W. V. Quine has remarked, "Meaning accrues primarily to whole sentences, and only derivatively to separate words. . . . We give the meaning of a sentence by explaining the sentence, and the meaning of a word by explaining how it works in sentences." Quine argues that a child initially learns sentences such as "It's raining" and "This is red" by "conditioning, unaided by auxiliary sentences," and then achieves higher levels of linguistic competence by analogies ("from the apparent role of a word in one sentence he guesses its role in another") and by noting how sentences are related to each other ("he discovers that people assent to a sentence of some one form only contingently upon assenting to a corresponding sentence of some related form").[8]

And the English sinologist Arthur Cooper adds an interesting historical perspective to these studies. There was in prehistory, Cooper says, an "original, natural (poetic) language" that was purely metaphorical. People used a limited number of often similar terms to express different needs and desires. Understanding what was being said therefore depended on the circumstances in which an utterance was made. More complex symbolic language, "the newer, artificial (logical) language," developed later. Cooper finds evidence for this development of language in the evolution of the written forms of Chinese. The earlier metaphorical form "is well illustrated," Cooper writes,

by a Chinese character with meanings now like "to retire to rest," but in ancient texts also "to go busily to and fro." The character 栖 [xī], which was "tree" plus "bird's nest" ["tree" 木 plus "west" 西 in modern usage], illustrated the metaphor lying behind both. Birds "nest" (go to roost) at sunset [from whence the modern usage of "west"] and "nest" (build, go to and from their nests) in spring. . . . Contexts would make it perfectly clear which sense was meant before the notion grew of "words" possessing meanings in themselves.[9]

Thus Cooper's account of the metaphorical nature of early forms of language seems similar to Margaret Donaldson's evidence that children first learn utterances and later specific words. This suggests that the rules of grammar may be acquired as utterances become more precise through the use of words with stable meanings, and that they are therefore derived from the examples of a language the child hears: the brain generalizes from limited samples.

However, many linguists would not agree with this approach. Noam Chomsky, for example, argues that we are born with genetically determined "mental organs," among them one specialized in language that contains specific "rule systems" that "cannot be derived from the data of experience by 'induction,' 'abstraction,' 'analogy,' or 'generalization,' in any reasonable sense of these terms, any more than the basic structure of the mammalian visual system is inductively derived from experience."

The brain, in Chomsky's view, could not use the samples of language a child hears to derive the rules necessary to produce grammatical sentences. The rules must, in some sense, be innate, for the samples are too impoverished for generalization to be possible. The continuity of mental structures such as language—the ways in which past experience with language is related to present and future experience—is established through largely innate mental structures or rules, which are similar for all human beings and which form the basis of a grammar that can generate an infinite number of sentences.[10]

In fact, Chomsky's argument receives considerable support from the work of David Hubel and Torsten Wiesel mentioned at the beginning of part 3. They described what they consider to be innate connections in the visual system where cells apparently respond to the presence of specific stimuli (a line at a forty-degree angle, for example) in a particular part of the visual field. Such cells, in their view, are innately determined to detect specific visual features (for example, lines with specific orientations), and Hubel and Wiesel suggested that a hierarchical arrangement of feature detectors could be the basis for the formation of more complex visual images in the brain. Innate connections and the rules implicit in them therefore determine the functioning of the visual system; in a larger sense innate mechanisms would be responsible for brain function in general. Just as we learn to see colors and objects of all shapes because of rules that are embedded in the nerve cell connections that make up the visual system of the brain, we learn to understand specific languages because of certain general rules embedded in the language centers of the brain that permit the derivation of the more specific rules of grammar of the language the child actually hears.

There are, however, important new biological discoveries that suggest, as does the work of Donaldson, Quine, and, in a sense, Cooper, that the brain does not have rules embedded in its connections. Rather, as our reevaluation of nineteenth-century neurology has already shown, the brain appears capable of creating its own generalizations about the world without either specific built-in programs or specific prestored information. It is the biological basis of this ability to generalize that is the subject of part 4.

Neural Darwinism: A New Approach to Memory and Perception

> The man with a good memory does not remember anything because he does not forget anything.
>
> —SAMUEL BECKETT, *Proust* (1931)

IN 1895, Sigmund Freud made his last attempt to explain the neurophysiological basis of brain function. His essay on the subject, "Project for a Scientific Psychology," was never published during his lifetime. We have learned much about the brain since 1895, yet no equally ambitious attempt has since been made to examine the broad implications of neuroscientific research for the functioning of the brain and for psychology. Recently, Gerald M. Edelman, director of The Neurosciences Institute at The Rockefeller University in New York, has proposed a new theory, one that gives us powerful reasons to revise our ideas about how we think, act, and remember.

Central to Freud's work is the connection between memory and the psychology of everyday life. He considered memory to be a permanent record of past events, a record that was anatomically separate from the brain mechanisms that are responsible for our ability to make sense of the world around us. As he wrote in the final chapter of *The Interpretation of Dreams*, "there are obvious difficulties involved in supposing that one and the same system can accurately retain modifications of its elements and yet remain perpetually open to the reception of fresh occasions for modifications. . . . [Therefore] we shall distribute these two functions on to different systems."[1]

On December 6, 1896, Freud wrote to his close friend Wilhelm Fliess:

As you know, I am working on the assumption that our psychical mechanism has come into being by a process of stratification: the material present in the form of memory-traces being subjected from time to time to a *re-arrangement* in accordance with fresh circumstances—to a *re-transcription*. Thus what is essentially new about my theory is the thesis that memory is present not once but several times over, that it is laid down in various species of indications.

In the same letter he wrote, "If I could give a complete account of the psychological characteristics of perception and of the [registrations of memory], I should have described a new psychology."[2]

Freud was acutely aware that recollections are often imperfect and fragmentary, and that they can and do alter perceptions. His theory attempts to explain how what he took to be perfect stores of memory are so transformed, arguing that memories cannot be released in their permanent form because the satisfactions and pleasures once associated with youthful impressions can no longer be experienced directly. Hence they reappear in dreams, but disguised and reworked. Ideas, Freud argued, become separated from associated emotions ("affects") and disappear from consciousness. The emotions become attached to apparently unrelated ideas, disguising their real meaning. And we often appear to forget the memories themselves. Repression, screen memories, latent dream content, the return of the repressed—all are mechanisms elaborated in Freud's theory to account for the ways in which fixed memories, however distorted and incomplete, can manifest themselves and affect our present view of the world. Freudian theory attempts to explain an apparent paradox: if we believe that memories are, by their very nature, permanently stored in the brain, why are they rarely recalled in their original form? It is the inaccuracy of recollection that Freudian psychology evokes so well. The reasons for this apparent inaccuracy may, however, be quite different from those that Freud suggested. In fact, the assumption that memories are in any sense part of a fixed record may be wrong.

If memory is a fixed record, neurophysiologists still cannot determine precisely where and how memories are stored. The hypothesis of a fixed record may have been formulated prematurely, before sufficient attention could be paid to the means by which we recognize objects and events. We are probably much better at recognition than we are at recollection. We recognize people despite changes wrought by aging, and we recognize personal items we have misplaced and photographs of places we have visited. We can recognize paintings by

A New Approach to Memory and Perception

Picasso as well as adept imitations of Picasso. When we recognize a painting we have never seen as a Picasso or as an imitation, we are doing more than recalling earlier impressions. We are categorizing: Picassos and fakes. Our recognition of paintings or of people is the recognition of a category, not of a specific item. People are never exactly what they were moments before, and objects are never seen in exactly the same way.

One possible explanation is that our capacity to remember is not for specific recall of an image stored somewhere in our brain. Rather, it is an ability to organize the world around us into categories, some general, some specific. When we speak of a stored mental image of a friend, *which* image or images are we referring to? The friend doing what, when and where? One reason why the search for memory molecules and specific information storage zones in the brain has so far been fruitless may be that they are just not there. Unless we can understand how we categorize people and things and how we generalize, we may never understand how we remember. Yet we do remember names, telephone numbers, words and their definitions. Are these not examples of items that must be stored in some kind of memory? Note that we generally recall names and telephone numbers in a particular context; each of our recollections is different, just as we use the same word in different sentences. These are categorical, not just specific, recollections.

Clinical Studies

The Sense of Time

Clinical neurologists have long been aware that brain disease can lead to severe alterations in memory, but they have yet to analyze deeply the nature of categorization. In a rare abnormality resulting from brain damage and known as *prosopagnosia*, patients lose the ability to identify the faces of friends and well-known public personalities. But they can recognize faces as faces. And while they cannot identify their own car or their own coat, they do recognize cars and clothing as such. They apparently can recall general categories but not specific items. Something similar may occur in some forms of amnesia as well. Antonio Damasio and his colleagues at the University of Iowa Medical School described a patient with amnesia, sitting in a room with the curtains drawn and unable to recall the season. When the patient pulled the curtain back and looked out the window, he noted the color of the trees and the dress of a passerby and exclaimed, "By golly, it must be July or August." He could not recall what month it was, but he could deduce it given appropriate evidence.

These studies appear to suggest that our ability to recognize general categories as opposed to specific items such as Mary's face or Alison's hat depends on two different brain functions. But the ability to recognize Alison's hat is, in part at least, based on temporal associations. We may have seen Alison wearing that hat last Sunday. The loss of the ability to categorize events in time can cause a nearly total loss of specific references. It is not that the specific item can no longer be recalled, but that its temporal order or its arrangement in succession has not been formed or has been lost. When Damasio and his colleagues questioned the man with amnesia about the calendar year, they found he had brain damage that made him unable to establish "temporal and spatial relationships between separate sensory information items."[3]

The sense of time itself is the consequence of our ability to establish a sequence for events, and this may depend on what is, or is not, recognized at a given moment. In 1895 the *British Medical Journal* reported the case of a railway engineer* who, following a serious head injury,

could not recognize his wife or his old comrades, and also [had] *difficulty in recognizing common objects* and their uses. Thus on one occasion he drank his own urine from a vessel, under the impression it was water, and several times he got pieces of ice out of his ice-cup, and declared they were sweetmeats. This failure to recognize—that is, to recall previous mental images for the purpose of comparison with present ones—was strikingly shown by his failure for weeks to recognize a fellow-workman who met with an accident, and was brought into hospital and placed in the bed next to him. But what was most remarkable was that *the whole of his life for twenty years before the accident was wiped out* from his memory. He asserted that he had never worked on the railway, and that he was a farm labourer. . . .

His reasoning processes were fairly orderly, but as, owing to the blanks in his memory, he often argued from false premises, he arrived at ludicrously incorrect conclusions. For example, he occupied one of the houses built by the railway company for their servants, and as he had no recollection of having

---

*This case is similar to that of H. M., who in the 1950s suffered a similar loss of memory following brain surgery. The case of H. M. is one of the best-known studies of memory loss following the surgical removal of brain tissue.[4]

worked for them for five or six years, he argued that he had no right to be there, and insisted with unnecessary warmth that his wife should pack up and leave the house before they got into trouble for being there.[5]

His failure to recognize that he was a legitimate occupant of the house was due not to an inability to recall when he had first moved in, or even for how long he had lived there, but rather to his having "forgotten" that he had worked for the railway company for the past several years. This is not a temporal loss, but an inability to relate the railway company to any period of his working life.

Claiming that twenty years of the patient's memory had been "wiped out" is therefore misleading. The patient cannot *correlate* certain pieces of information, such as his employment with his presence in the house, and this gives the illusion of a memory loss of large blocks of time. What he lost was not time but the way events and objects were related. Even his having forgotten that he had once been employed by the railway company may have resulted from an inability to relate to that company the various jobs he had held during his life. Indeed, in the presence of his co-workers, he was able to recall some events relating to that period of his employment: "This partial return of memory seems to have been in part due to the habit of his 'mates' coming in and talking to him of the past, and continually reminding him of occurrences which were likely to have made an impression on him."[6]

The setting (the presence of his mates) reordered the events in the railway worker's life. Time is not an absolute quality in memory; it is an ordering of people, places, things, and events. There are no calendars in the brain.

166

A New Approach to Memory and Perception

Penfield's Memory "Flashbacks" and Emotions

The neurosurgeon Wilder Penfield thought he had discovered conclusive evidence of permanent memories in the brain in 1933 when, during an operation on a patient who was fully conscious, he electrically stimulated the brain surface and the patient, much to his own and Penfield's surprise, had a memory "flashback." As Penfield described such flashbacks after years of study:

The flashback responses to electrical stimulation . . . bear no relation to present experience in the operating room. Consciousness for the moment is doubled, and the patient can discuss the phenomenon. If he is hearing music, he can hum in time to it. The astonishing aspect of the phenomenon is that suddenly he is aware of all that was in his mind during an earlier strip of time. It is the stream of a former consciousness flowing again. If music is heard, it may be orchestra or voice or piano. Sometimes he is aware of all he was seeing at the moment; sometimes he is aware only of the music. It stops when the electrode is lifted. It may be repeated (even many times) if the electrode is replaced without too long a delay. This electrical recall is completely at random. Most often, the event was neither significant nor important.[7]

The flashbacks were characteristically dreamlike: "I keep having dreams . . . I keep seeing things—I keep dreaming of things." Yet the "memories" were often observations of *other* people doing things the patient was unlikely to have witnessed, as, for example, the boy who recognized his aunt's voice as his mother spoke with her and "was telling my aunt to come up and visit us tonight"; or the woman who suddenly saw herself during birth, apparently feeling that she was reliving the experience of being born; or the woman who "remembered" an experience in a lumberyard where she had never been: "Yes, I hear the same familiar sounds, it seems to be a woman calling. The same lady. That was not in the neighborhood. It seemed to be at the lumberyard."[8]

In fact, of the 520 patients who received electrical stimulation in the temporal lobes, the area of the brain where Penfield believed these memories were stored, only 40 produced what he called "experiential responses." Subsequent studies have shown that such experiential responses occur only when the limbic structures (generally believed to be essential for emotional experiences) are activated. As Pierre Gloor and his colleagues in Montreal noted in 1982: "Our observations on 35 epileptic patients . . . provide *prima facie* evidence that unless limbic structures are activated, either in the course of a spontaneous seizure or through artificial electrical stimulation, experiential phenomena do not occur." And in a description that gives compelling evidence for Freud's claim that memories without affect are unrecognizable (see pages 72–73), Pierre Gloor and his colleagues state:

The observation that such responses can be more easily elicited by stimulating at the limbic than at the neocortical "end" of this system suggests that limbic activation may be essential for bringing to a conscious level percepts elaborated by the temporal neocortex. One may conjecture that whatever we experience with our senses, particularly in the visual and auditory modalities, even after it has been elaborated as a percept in temporal neocortex, must ultimately be transmitted to limbic structures in order to assume experiential immediacy. *Attaching some affective or motivational significance to a percept may be the specific limbic contribution to this process. This may be the precondition for the percept to be consciously experienced or recalled and may imply that all consciously perceived events must assume some kind of affective dimension, if only ever so slight.*[9] [Italics added.]

Emotions are essential for creating and categorizing memories. Indeed, the sensations of both perception and recollection apparently require limbic activity. "It is well known that . . . inactivation of limbic structures produces automatism, confusion, and amnesia."[10]

But limbic activation alone, though it adds affect and may be responsible for the ordering of recollections, does not suffice for a true sensation of memory. Recollections remain fragmentary, as Freud had noted in dreams and neuroses long ago. Only upon awakening, or through an analytic reworking of one's thoughts and emotions—that is, by establishing an immediate context—can these fragmentary sensations become "memories." Reviewing Penfield's work, two American psychologists wrote in 1980:

There is good reason to believe that such reports [of memory flashbacks] may result from reconstruction of fragments of past experience or from constructions created at the time of report that bear little or no resemblance to past experience. Furthermore, secondary sources and popular accounts tend to distort the evidence so as to lend more credence to the notion of memory permanence than is really warranted. . . .

In sum, Penfield would have us believe that stimulation of the brain "causes previous experience to return to the mind of a conscious patient" and that "there is within the adult brain a remarkable record of the stream of each individual's awareness or consciousness." But these conclusions (and the video-recorder model), based as they are on the dubious protocols of a handful of patients, seem unwarranted. A reconstruction or construction hypothesis seems much more viable. A hint as to what is likely to go into such reconstructions was provided by

Mahl, Rothenberg, Delgado, and Hamlin in their examination of a 27-year-old housewife who underwent brain stimulation; they concluded that a strong determinant of the content of these "memories" is "the patient's mental content at the time of stimulation." These so-called memories, then, appear to consist merely of the thoughts and ideas that happened to exist just prior to and during the stimulation.[11]

Limbic system activity (emotions) links the *ambiguous* fragments of "memory" into more coherent wholes that can be related to the immediate setting. There are no symbols in the brain; there are patterns of activity, fragments, which acquire different meanings in different contexts. What Penfield discovered were not memories, but these fragments that Freud had better understood.

Individual needs and desires, then, determine how we classify the people, places, and events that fill our daily lives. Moreover, the categories we use seem to depend on cross-correlations, or context. Yet many influential theories of mental function posit fixed entities that exist independently. Freud, for example, described many ordinary objects as fitting into categories based on their resemblance to male or female sexual organs (phallic symbols, for example), and tended to view such categories as representing deeper drives that are universal within the human species. Many clinical neurologists and psychologists disagree with Freud's notion of universal sexual drives; they nevertheless hold that information is organized into permanent categories in one or more memory systems within the brain, and that it can systematically be brought to consciousness in ways analogous to memory searches used in computers. The processes that are responsible for our recognition of categories, however, do not seem to depend on such fixed mechanisms.

The Biological View

Darwin

There are good biological reasons to question the idea of fixed universal categories. In a broad sense, they run counter to the principles of the Darwinian theory of evolution. Darwin stressed that populations are collections of unique individuals. In the biological world there is no typical animal or typical plant. When we say a salt molecule has a specific size, we are giving a measurement that, allowing for error, is true for all salt molecules. But there is no set of measurements that will universally describe more than the one example of plant or animal we are measuring. Qualities we associate with human beings and other animals are abstractions invented by us that miss the nature of the biological variation. The central conception in Darwinian thought is that variations in populations occur from which selection may take place. It is the variation, not the mean, that is real. It was Darwin's recognition of this profound difference between the biological and physical worlds that led to the rise of modern biology. The mechanisms of inheritance through genes create diversity within populations; selection from these populations allows certain organisms to survive in unpredictable environments.

Darwinian ideas have had a variable influence on psychological thinking, which has sometimes strayed from biological explanation. Modern ethology, which studies the relation of animal to human behavior, has recaptured much of the Darwinian flavor that unfortunately left psychology when early learning theorists such as Pavlov seemed to explain behavior successfully without paying heed to the differences among animal species. But as important as their insights are, ethologists have not applied Darwinian thinking to the workings of the brain in each individual of a species.

Does evolutionary thought have anything to do with the explanation of the psychology of individual human beings? The theory of the brain that Gerald Edelman proposed in 1978 sought to explain neurophysiological function as a Darwinian system involving variation and selection. Although his theory is confined to neurobiology, implicit in this work is a bold attempt to unify the biological and psychological sciences, one that strongly depends on the ideas of evolution and the facts of developmental biology.

The Immune System

Edelman had earlier studied the immune system. For years, scientists had wondered how the body produced antibodies against viruses or bacteria it had never encountered. Linus Pauling had suggested in 1940 that there was one basic kind of antibody molecule in the body. When the body was invaded by a bacterium, he had argued, the antibody molecule would mold itself around the intruder, thus acquiring a definite shape. Copies of the mold were made and released into the bloodstream where they would bind to the invading bacteria. The system *learned*, or was instructed by, the shape of a bacterium only after being exposed to it.

Pauling's theory of just one kind of antibody protein proved to be wrong. In 1969 Edelman and his colleagues worked out the complete chemical structure of the antibody molecule, providing the important clue to what structures within the molecule are varied to produce the millions of different kinds of antibodies needed to protect the body against foreign organisms. For this work he won the Nobel Prize in 1972, along with the late Rodney Porter of England. Their studies confirmed a theory suggested in the 1950s by MacFarlane Burnet and Niels Jerne that all animals are born with a complete repertoire of antibodies and that intruding bacteria *select* those antibodies that can effectively combat their presence.

Contrary to Pauling's theory, the presence of the bacterium does not determine the nature of the antibody that is made, but only the amount. A limited number of genes, a few hundred or a few thousand at most, provide, through recombinatory mechanisms, the codes for the many millions of different antibodies. Specialized cells in the blood each produce one of the many kinds of possible antibodies that then become attached to the cell surface. An antibody molecule that happens to fit more or less closely a virus or bacterium floating in the bloodstream will bind itself to the virus or bacterium. This sets off a chain of events that causes the cell to divide and make thousands of copies of itself (clones) and more of the same kind of antibody. Other cells may carry antibody molecules that fit the virus or bacterium in different ways, and these cells, too, will bind to the virus or bacterium and produce clones. The body can rid itself of a virus or bacterium only if there is at least one good fit in its antibody repertoire. Usually there are several fits and some of them may overlap.

So the immunological system is not taught what antibodies it has to make to rid the body of a particular virus. The invading virus *selects* the appropriate antibodies, and these will be different in each individual. An unfortunate organism may not have any antibodies in its repertoire that can bind the virus, and this could be fatal. Scientists have generally been pleased with this solution to the immunological question because it is consistent with the Darwinian principles of selection that formed the basis of modern biology. Theories of immunology based on a process of learning or instruction are not.

The Brain

Comparison of these findings on immunology to the theory of evolution suggested to Edelman that the brain, too, may function as a selective system and that what we call learning is really a form of selection. The theory he worked out is based on three fundamental claims: (1) during the development of the brain in the embryo, a highly variable and individual pattern of connections is formed between brain cells (neurons); (2) after birth, a pattern of neural connections is fixed in each individual, but certain combinations of connections are selected over others as a result of the stimuli the brain receives through the senses; (3) such selection would occur particularly in groups of brain cells that are connected in sheets, or "maps," and these maps "speak" to one another back and forth to create categories of things and events.[12]

But is there a mechanism that creates such diversity in each brain? In 1963, the Nobel Prize–winning neurologist Roger Sperry, working on the origin of visual maps, proposed that the billions of complicated connections in the brain are each determined by specific chemical markers on each neuron. In this view, particular genes presumably provide a code for each of the markers. Twins with identical genes therefore should have identical, or nearly identical, brains. Sperry's model may not have claimed that learning is preprogrammed, but it does seem to imply that what a person can learn is limited by predetermined connections in his or her brain. If Sperry were right, many brain functions would be genetically determined, and to this extent organisms could be limited in their ability to adapt to new environments. Adaptive behavior and flexibility would have to arise by instruction; that is, by external stimuli creating patterns in the brain, much as programs give instructions to computers. Yet we know that animals can adapt individually to different environments. The human brain has permitted survival in remarkably varied circumstances throughout history. Genetic determinism strains credibility because it makes it difficult to account for the enormous variability of thought and action.

For Edelman, the important issue was not, as Sperry had argued, how specific structures in the brain are made according to markers on each neuron, but how, given a particular set of genes, enough variability could be created within the constant overall structure of the brain to allow for the adaptability of humans and higher animals in an unpredictable environment. The deeper issue that had to be explored to understand this was the relationship between genes, on the one hand, and, on the other, the form and structure—or "morphology"—of animals. Notwithstanding all the work on the genetic code, biologists still cannot predict the shape of an organism from the information in its genes. If dinosaur genes rather than dinosaur bones had been found, we would never have known they were dinosaurs and could not have said what they looked like. Why don't genes tell us about morphology?

CAMs: Context and History in Embryology

The answer to the preceding question, according to Edelman's findings, lies in early embryonic development. As an embryo develops, cells divide, move from place to place, and ultimately become specialized. A cell's fate, whether it will become a liver cell or a nerve cell, depends on where it happens to be at the moment when specialization begins, as well as where it has been. Cell shapes and movements will inevitably vary in each individual, making it impossible to predict exactly where a particular cell will be at a given time. The genetic mechanisms that determine what a cell will become must somehow be sensitive to its location at a particular time. If each cell's specialization were completely predetermined by genes, even one misplaced cell could create havoc and the organism's subsequent development would follow an abnormal course. A supporting beam that is put into place just moments too late is of no use once the walls have collapsed.

How does a pattern emerge in the embryo from early activity of the cells? Biological systems are not built from preformed parts. Instead cells are cemented together in the embryo, and the individual cells or groups of cells are then shaped into structures that serve more complex functions. In determining the shape, it is the signals across the boundaries of such structures that count. How this works may be suggested by an analogy.

Imagine an architect given the task of shaping a brick wall into the facade of a building, with windows, ornaments, and a main door. One way our architect may proceed is to indicate where the holes for the windows would be drilled by drawing the borders on the brick wall. The holes drilled and the window frames added, he might then add indications for the shutter hinges on the window frames. In general, shaping a relatively uniform collection of interconnected material units, such as bricks, into a well-differentiated structure requires determining the *boundaries* of the structures that have to be carved into the units or added to them. And those boundaries can be determined only after all the bricks (or other material subunits) are in place. One brick might be substituted for another without changing the pattern. Above all, the boundaries will determine the function of the different bricks, such as whether they will support a window or frame a doorway.

Similarly, as tissue grows in the embryo, borders are formed demarcating the different functional parts of the organism; but obviously there is no architect overseeing the procedure. The borders are established between different groups of cells by different intercellular cements or glues, known as cell adhesion molecules, or CAMs. Three kinds of CAMs were discovered by Edelman and his colleagues in the late 1970s, and more have since been found. Two of the CAMs appear on the surfaces of cells very early in embryonic development. One is called L-CAM because it was first discovered in the liver, and the other is N-CAM, since it was originally found in association with nerves. L-CAMs on the cell surface will stick only to other L-CAMs on the cell surface, and the same is true of N-CAMs; L-CAMs and N-CAMs will not stick to each other. For these primary CAMs, cells can adhere to each other only when they have the same kind of CAMs on their surfaces.

The structure of the cell adhesion molecules themselves is determined by particular genes. And in early development of the embryo, other genes regulate when the CAMs are produced. The exact amount and "stickiness" of the CAMs (which vary continuously as the embryo develops), however, depend on the present and past position of the cells carrying them, and the individual cell's position is not under direct genetic control. Therefore the arrangement of groups of cells that are linked together by one kind of CAM will vary even in genetically identical individuals. These groups of cells send signals that turn CAM genes on and off, as well as turning on and off the action of genes that specify cell specialization. The entire sequence by which differentiation occurs is determined not directly by genes but indirectly by the combined action of genes and signals from cell groups that activate genes, and is therefore called *epigenetic*.

Cells linked together in collectives by L-CAMs form borders with other cells linked together in other collectives by N-CAMs. The borders result because the two kinds of molecules do not stick to each other. Edelman and his colleagues have shown that cells on one side of the border will subsequently change into more specialized cells of one kind, and those on the other side of the border will become specialized cells of another kind. Throughout embryonic development, borders are formed between cells that are linked together with different CAMs, and following border formation the cells specialize. As the cells differentiate further, new CAM borders are formed before new changes are introduced by signals from the cell groups to the genes that activate both CAMs and the genes that specify cell specialization. Depending on the past history of the two cell groups, signals exchanged at the border between collections of

A New Approach to Memory and Perception

N-CAM and L-CAM cells will determine the subsequent formation of very different kinds of cells on each side of the border.

The function of the border between cell groups with different CAMs thus depends on the context: the surrounding cells, and the past history of the cells. In general, moreover, the rules governing CAM response are similar both for the neurons of the brain and for other body structures. Because the borders of cell collectives depend on dynamics of movement, there will be individual variations that are not determined just by genes and whose diversity will ensure that different brains will have different structures. Yet the general patterns formed and the broadly similar sequences of embryonic development would explain the fact that the individual brains of members of a species resemble one another.

The importance of the borders formed by the CAM-linked collectives was shown in a spectacular series of experiments in Edelman's laboratory on the emergence of a single feather in the chicken. At each stage in the feather's morphogenesis, borders were found between groups of cells linked together with different kinds of CAMs. Following the formation of the borders, each group of cells changed, those on one side into one kind of cell and those on the other into another kind of cell. For example, the final feather, with its regular pattern of branching (a pattern that varies from feather to feather), is carved out of a cylinder of tissue. The distinctive feather pattern arises after alternating groups of cells (that is, L-CAM–linked cell groups alternating with N-CAM–linked cell groups) make their appearance. Groups of cells with N-CAM linkages then die, while the alternating groups with L-CAM linkages become hardened, or keratinized. The result: a feather. The edges of the barbs on the feather are the borders between the L- and N-CAM cell groups. Even more dramatically, when changes were induced experimentally in the linkages made by one kind of CAM, cell groups that were linked by a completely different kind of CAM were altered so that scale-like structures, rather than feather-like structures, emerged.[13]

From the workings of such epigenetic mechanisms, we can see why knowing the entire genetic repertoire of an animal would not alone permit us to predict its final detailed morphology. Identical twins are never absolutely identical. And just as every feather has a different pattern of branching, every brain would be expected to have a different pattern of connections.

The demonstration that there are molecular reasons why no two brains could be identical is central to Edelman's view that the brain functions as a system based on selection—the CAM mechanism creates diversity in the anatomical connections of an individual's brain, which has enormous numbers of cells and connections. The context and history of cellular development thus largely determine the structure of the brain; and therefore context and history are also important in brain function. Because development, structure, and function are related, it would not be surprising if the functional activities of a connected group of cells in the brain were found to depend both on the activities of neighboring cell groups and on the past history of the particular group itself.

A New Approach to Memory and Perception

Edelman's Theory of Neuronal Group Selection

To show that brain function, like structure, depends on context and history and not on localized functions and fixed memories is the burden of Edelman's theory of neuronal group selection. What emerges is a new approach to the biological basis of psychology.

A major claim of this approach is that the unit of selection in the brain is a neuronal group, a set of interconnected neurons that function together. The patterns of connections that are established among neurons vary from group to group because of the changes in dynamics of the CAMs during development. The brain thus contains large numbers of different neuronal groups.

Neuronal groups are connected to one another as well as to the sensory receptors for light, touch, and sound in the eyes, skin, and ears. In general, neighboring groups of neurons in the brain receive input from neighboring sensory receptors (for example, on the second and third fingers of the hand); two neighboring groups in the brain can in fact receive input from the same sensory receptor. Although the inputs can overlap, the responses of each group to the stimuli will be different. Because each group of neurons has its own pattern of internal connections, which differs from those of other groups, each group will respond differently, even to identical stimuli.

The activities of a group of interconnected neurons would acquire significance not just because of the anatomical connections and physiological mechanisms on which the functioning of that group depends, but because of its context and the history of its received signals as well. If this is true, then a given "memory" cannot be stored in a specific place in the brain, since neighboring activities would of necessity change and therefore the "context" of any neuronal cell group is never constant. If one were to assume that a memory was in fact stored as it is in a computer, altering this process would irreparably destroy it.

The embryonic processes I have described involving CAMs are central in creating a large repertoire of different neuronal groups. But after birth the principle of selection changes. Instead of alterations of CAMs, changes in the *strength* but not the *pattern* of connections occur; such changes determine the paths over which neural signals will flow.* Environmental stimuli may cause one group to respond with greater activity than other groups receiving the same input. And when this happens, laboratory experiments show that the connections between the neurons in that group (the synaptic junctions) can be strengthened.

Edelman and his colleagues have worked out a set of rules that might govern these synaptic alterations. Molecular changes take place within neurons and at the synaptic junctions, so that the neurons tend to be activated by similar stimuli on subsequent occasions. Particular variants within the brain's population of neuronal groups are *selected* by the stimulus. Indeed, a group that responds to a stimulus might do more than this. As its connections are strengthened it might alter the strength of its links to other groups and, by *competing* with other groups, integrate neurons from them into its own response activity. The strengthening of the synap-

---

*This is analogous to the process by which antibodies that have been selected are then produced in large numbers, or cloned. The two processes resemble each other in effect, but the mechanisms are different: in the brain the strengths of synaptic connections are increased; in the immune system the number of cells is increased through cloning.

tic connections creates what Edelman calls a secondary repertoire, made up of neuronal groups that respond better to specific stimuli because they have been selected and their connections strengthened.

In their responses to stimuli, neuronal groups could be likened to a set of radio receivers, each tuned to a small band of frequencies. One radio might receive frequencies in the 1600 to 1700 kilocycle range, and another might receive frequencies in the 1550 to 1650 kilocycle range. Depending on the broadcast frequencies in the area, some of the receivers will respond to one broadcast, others to several broadcasts, and others to none at all. Analogously to an animal moving its head or body, moving from New York to Peking, for example, would change the response patterns of the individual receivers. The receiver's purpose depends on where it is: in Peking it receives Radio Peking; in New York, WCBS; and in Moscow, Radio Free Europe, Radio Moscow, and a lot of jamming simultaneously.

Like the radio receivers, a given neuronal group can respond to more than one stimulus—what is called a *degenerate response*. In our analogy, a given radio receiver might pick up Radio Peking better than Radio Moscow, but it can pick up either station. (Of course, stimuli are not organized into coherent pieces of information like radio broadcasts. At higher levels in the brain, the stimuli must be organized in ways that will be meaningful and useful for the organism.)

Brain Maps

The brain performs this organizing operation by using maps made up of neuronal groups. A map is a collection of neuronal groups in the brain which are arranged in a way that preserves the pattern of relationships either between a sheet of sensory receptors (such as those in the skin of the hand) and a sheet of neural tissue in the brain to which the sensory stimuli have been transmitted, or between two sheets of neural tissue. Groups are arranged in maps that "speak" back and forth to one another so as to create categories of things and events. Different kinds of maps are found in different parts of the brain, and an analysis of how such maps interact— their interactions are called *reentry*—is an essential and final part of Edelman's theory.

Because the brain has to be prepared for unpredictable events, it must map stimuli in a variety of ways. Brain maps sort incoming stimuli by similarity (same frequency of sound, same intensity of sound, and so on) as well as by a mixture of properties. The main evolutionary principle at work here is that stimuli are organized into patterns that will help the organism cope with its environment.

In 1870 two young Germans, Gustav Theodor Fritsch and Eduard Hitzig, first discovered that the brain maps motor stimuli. They reported that touching discrete areas of a dog's brain activated specific parts of its body. By the end of the century, motor and sensory maps were a well-established feature of neuroanatomical teaching. These maps were assumed to be permanent and more or less identical in all members of a species.

It was therefore surprising when, in 1983, Michael Merzenich and his collaborators at the University of California at San Francisco discovered that sensory maps in the brains of normal monkeys showed considerable variation. The brain maps in a particular monkey's brain varied over time. And there was considerable variation in corresponding maps in different monkeys as well. Subsequent experiments demonstrated that the maps became rearranged, even within short periods of time, following injury to a nerve supplying sensory input from one of the monkey's fingers.

Merzenich's work gives powerful support to Edelman's claim that particular combinations of neuronal groups are selected competitively from the general population of neuronal groups by sensory input. Since the nerves from the different areas of the skin of the hand are connected by overlapping branches to the same receiving areas in the brain, the part of the skin surface represented in a particular brain by a group of neurons depends on selective competition. Neuronal groups in one area of the brain may, for example, receive overlapping input from both the back and the palm of the hand, and the stimuli from the palm may more effectively select particular neuronal groups, establishing a dominant representation of the palm of the hand in the map in that part of the brain. Should the incoming nerves be damaged, reducing or eliminating the input from the palm (as in Merzenich's experiments), the groups that could respond to the stimuli from the back of the hand would then be able to be expressed in the absence of competition from the neuronal groups in the palm. Thus, based on the inherent variation among neuronal groups, a new representation emerges in that area of the brain. The continuity of the new map's general activity nonetheless can still represent, in some abstracted form, the activity at the sensory receptors.

Information in the brain is distributed among many maps, and, according to Edelman's theory, there must be incessant reference back and forth, or reentry, among them for categorization to occur. Sounds, for example, can be categorized as speech, noise, or music; or they can be used to locate things in space. Recent research shows that such localization requires a number of interacting maps. Owls, like human beings, use sounds to locate moving animals, for instance, a mouse they might attack. The important sensory clues are the different arrival times of a sound at each ear, and its intensity. Since the owl's brain cannot directly map the different times of arrival of a sound at each ear, two initial sensory maps represent the frequencies heard by the owl: one maps those heard in the right ear, and the other maps those heard in the left ear. These representations are then combined in another map where the arrival times (called *sound disparities*) of a given frequency in one ear are compared with those in the other ear.

The sounds made by a mouse in a field can by this means be categorized according to the disparities in sound. These disparities can be used to help determine the sources of sounds. Specific neuronal groups, or neurons, within a map may be activated by a difference in arrival time between the two ears of, for example, one-thousandth of a second. In itself the activity of the neurons will not tell the owl's brain the source of the sound. But the entire pattern of activity of the map, the ways in which other neurons are activated as well, will represent in the owl's brain the location of the source of the sound. This pattern will have to be extracted in a further mapping, which could for example characterize certain patterns of activity indicating that sources of sound were, say, at 30 degrees to the left, others at 60 degrees to the right, and so on. Finally, the mapping that has located the source of the sound is connected to a visual map of space, created from the owl's visual receptors. The visual map is thus related to a map that recategorizes auditory sensory input to place sounds in space. By relating the two sensory modalities, the owl's brain creates a general map (auditory and visual) of space and the owl can re-spond to a variety of sensory inputs.

A particular pattern of activity will lead to a motor response in which the owl dives for its prey. If the owl is successful, it will associate that mapping and that pat-tern of activity with the particular motor act of attack-ing. If it fails, however, it will try other responses until it finally succeeds in capturing its prey. This was shown in a series of experiments by Eric I. and Phyllis F. Knudsen in which young owls were raised with one ear plugged, thus shifting the perceived location of sound relative to its actual location. In four to six weeks these owls learned to localize sound accurately. They had ap-parently adjusted to the altered mapping of sound by rearranging their internal mappings. Recognition there-fore depends on mapped and remapped patterns of activity.

No single map contains all the information necessary for an owl's movements, and, as I have said, there must be a constant reference back and forth from neurons in one map to neurons in the other by means of so-called reentrant connections—that is, nerves traveling in both directions to link the maps, in each of which neuronal selection is taking place. According to Edelman's theory, this is how the brain creates its categories and generaliza-tions. Of course, the owl brain may also use the initial mapping of sound frequencies for higher maps that rep-resent not spatial disparities but rather the actual se-quence of sounds (to identify the kind of animal making the noise, perhaps). This will eventually create other kinds of categories for sound information.

The brain has many different kinds of maps and ways of mapping other maps that categorize "inputs" in many ways. The purpose of the maps is to create perceptual categorizations that will permit the animal to act in appropriate ways.* The environments in which an animal might find itself will of course change, and so the perceptual categories must also change. But this is exactly what the multiple mappings are best suited for: the maps interact with one another and constantly recategorize information. And by referring the more abstract mappings back to the primary sensory maps that have a continuous relationship with external stimuli, the brain can effectively keep track of its various regroupings of the sensory inputs.

We dream when the maps are released from the constraints of sensory order during sleep. The fluidity of the memory traces—the fact that the activity of a particular neuronal group or set of neuronal groups never represents any specific item or person or event—is evident from the fact that the ways in which dreams recombine faces, words, and events can greatly vary from dream to dream and can be interpreted in different ways at different times. Our memories are organized when we are confronted by environmental stimuli, when we are fully awake. They must be, or our responses would not be appropriate to the given circumstances.

That mappings can be related to one another without any preestablished instructions has been demonstrated by Edelman and his colleague George Reeke, Jr., who built a new kind of automaton, based on the principles of selection, to simulate the mapping activity of the brain. The automaton abstracted from the mappings of

*The origin of perceptual categories by neuronal group selection is in some ways analogous to the origin of species by natural selection. Much as unpredictable events over a long period may result in the selection of certain characteristics in organisms, unpredictable environmental events in an animal's lifetime may result in the selection of certain neuronal groups leading to the formation of perceptual categories.

visual inputs a variety of categorizations, such as for letters of the alphabet, without having been given specific instructions. This activity provided further evidence that interacting maps are essential for categorizing perceptions in a selective system.

"Darwin II": A New Approach to Machine Simulations of Recognition

The automaton is the first man-made device that strictly adheres to the most sophisticated neurophysiological knowledge of our day, and an examination of its functioning provides a sharp contrast to the computational and PDP approaches previously discussed.

Darwin II, an automaton constructed in Edelman's laboratory in the early 1980s, consists of a screen on which figures are projected in white and black patterns. Like a collection of sensory receptors, the screen is divided into a grid, with each square within the grid projected onto grids in a second panel in a network system called "Darwin." Each panel in the first grid projects to the equivalent panel in the second grid, but the panels in the second grid contain "feature detectors"—that is, they respond to lines, or corners, with a specific orientation. The second panel, therefore, indicates the presence or absence of a particular feature in the first grid. This is similar to the feature detectors that Hubel and Wiesel found in the visual cortex (see part 3). In figure 4.1, the various features of an A will be activated in the second array in exactly the same positions as they appear on the input array. If the A is turned on its side on the input array, an A will appear on its side in the second panel.

There is nothing very surprising about the feature detectors in the second panel. It is known that something like feature detectors exists in the brain, and it has gener-

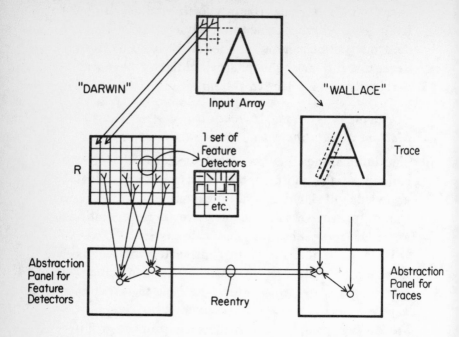

Figure 4.1.

Darwin II. The patterns of activity in the lower left and right panels represent abstractions of the activity in the middle-level Darwin and Wallace panels, respectively. Thus the pattern of activity, at any given moment, in the lower left-hand panel represents, in an abstract way, the feature detector activity in the Darwin panel at that time. Similarly the activity in the lower right-hand panel represents, also in an abstract way, the tracing activity (boundaries and continuity) in the Wallace panel. Simultaneous activity in the two lower panels strengthens the connections between the active groups in each panel. These strengthened connections are called *reentry,* and they permit generalizations to emerge.

SOURCE: Adapted from George N. Reeke, Jr., and Gerald M. Edelman, "Selective Networks and Recognition Automata," *Annals of the New York Academy of Sciences* 426 (1984): 189.

ally been assumed, both by neurophysiologists and workers in artificial intelligence, that it is important for reconstructing the initial image on the retina. The individual features could be fitted together into a whole.

A New Approach to Memory and Perception

Early vision machines built on these principles had to be given much extra information in order to avoid many of the ambiguities normally present in a visual scene. Recognizing this problem, David Marr, as we saw in part 3, developed a more general approach, deriving from the initial input array not features but variations in intensity. The point of the Darwin II feature detectors is to show not that feature detection is necessary for perceiving shapes, but rather that features can form the basis of a variety of perceptual categories.

Groups in a third panel are connected to several groups in the second panel, so that the third-panel response represents, in an abstract way, a whole pattern of activity in the second panel. One group in the third panel might be activated by a pattern of activity that includes four squares in the second panel. (Of course, shifting the stimulus in the input array will alter the pattern of activity of the second panel and, consequently, of the third as well.)

The third panel, then, samples collections of features of objects, each sampling being independent of the others. There is no way of predetermining what goes with what in the environment. Spelke, it will be remembered (see part 3), found that infants associated two different objects of different colors, which were apparently attached and moving together. Stationary, uniformly colored rods, partly occluded in the middle, were taken for *two* objects. Darwin II tries to duplicate this fundamental fact: we perceive the world without labels, and we can label it only when we have decided how its features should be organized. Just as the infant does not necessarily organize the world according to color, shape, and texture, but rather may associate two colors with the same moving object, Darwin II does not predetermine how the features that make up the visual environment must be organized.

Ultimately, an infant's perception appears to be organized in terms of moving boundaries of objects, a *spatio-temporal* correlation that Darwin II attempts to capture in the second parallel network, known as "Wallace." Wallace uses a tracing mechanism, analogous to the movement of the hands, to determine the outlines of an object, its contours or continuity. Thus the features being detected in the Darwin network are correlated in the Wallace network. The Darwin system (analogous to the visual system) might detect corners and oriented lines of various kinds, and map these features in a variety of ways on the third panel. At the same time, the Wallace network (like the tactile system) notes the continuous relationships of the boundaries. Wallace is sensitive to the presence of lines and junctions of lines, largely ignoring lengths and orientations. (For example, it responds to an upright A and a sideways A in a similar way.) The Wallace network therefore responds to different As (short fat ones, or tall thin ones) with similar responses. And as in the Darwin network, these tracings are abstracted in a third panel which represents different patterns of activities of the tracing mechanism.

The Wallace network is activated in similar ways by objects that have related shapes, though the objects may be oriented differently in space. The network classifies objects by their continuity properties, though, of course, the brain's tactile system could equally well classify objects by similarity of texture.

Since the third panels (the panels that "abstract" the feature detector responses or the tactile-continuity responses) are connected, a new property of the system emerges—generalization—and becomes possible because of the reentrant connections between the abstraction panels. An active "feature-abstraction group" will cause the strengthening of connections to an active "feature-correlation group," thereby associating the two responses. This "coupling" of different kinds of mapping permits generalization. And it is this very coupling of maps and of mappings of maps within the brain by continual selection that Edelman's theory of Neural Darwinism claims as the basis for the brain's ability to generalize. (See appendix C.)

There is no sense in which the response of a group in Darwin II can be associated with a specific stimulus, any more than a stimulus can be "associated" with another stimulus in a simple way. Recognition of an object requires its categorization. And categories are created by *coupling*, or correlating different samplings of the stimuli. This is best achieved through mappings that create a variety of possible groupings of the stimuli, and relating different mappings to each other through reentry, or cross-correlations. Indeed, the groups that respond to a stimulus in Darwin II do so because they have been *selected*. When a particular stimulus activates a set of groups on several occasions, the strengths of its connections are increased, making them more likely to respond on subsequent exposures to the stimulus. But the responses of the groups are "degenerate"—that is, since they can respond to more than one kind of stimulus, no response to a particular stimulus will be exactly the same every time. In Darwin II every "recollection" is, in a sense, a new creation.

Unlike the generalizations and categorizations that have been achieved with PDP networks, Darwin II requires no decisions about the kinds of information it must process. PDP networks can process words and, to some extent, sentences: that words and sentences are the information being sought has already been decided by the constructors of the machines. But how does the organism decide which sounds are words and which are foghorns, bleating sheep, or whatever? Sounds must be sampled in many ways—mapped and remapped and cross-correlated—and then those abstractions that represent phonemes, words, and sentences must themselves be interrelated. There are, however, various layers of mappings here, and it is not clear how they relate to one another. Words and sentences are the consequences of the interactions of many maps and mappings of maps in a very general sense. The brain must generalize and categorize sound patterns first as words, and the ways in which it achieves these categorizations will affect how words are subsequently mapped. One cannot separate the one task—deriving, for example, words from sounds—from the further task of learning, for example, the past tense of verbs. The very creation of words is part and parcel of the creation of the past tense. It is the entire pattern of activity of the brain, the mappings and the reentries, that represents the information. The tasks cannot be parceled into those for the formation of phonemes and those for the formation of words. What appear to be specialized functional units (modules) are the various abstractions created by multiple interconnected maps. But the *principles* responsible for the formation of these abstractions—the mappings, the reentry, and the related motor activity—are the same whether the abstraction be a category of phonemes or of words. In the modular view, functional specialization implies different principles of operation for each module. In the view being argued here, different categorizations are different *procedures,* but the fundamental principles of categorization are the same.

A New Approach to Memory and Perception

The continuity of mental function requires that information be related in time to new pieces of information. This is possible only if the *sources* of that information, the sensory stimuli that are being sampled and abstracted in a variety of ways, can be constantly related to its various transformations from map to map. Only by constantly referring back to the initial mapping of the sensory stimuli can the information be given any spatiotemporal continuity. But this implies that the activity of the entire network of maps in a particular environmental setting tells us what information is being created. Indeed, the brain must make sense of the sensory stimuli, and the ways in which it does so depend on a variety of environmental factors. Hence, it must use selection of neuronal groups in its operations. There is no knowing in what ways the stimuli will be relevant as the environment changes.

A set of movements, for example, can be effective only if they are related to the position of the body and its surroundings. And, of course, as the movements are in progress, they must be constantly referred to the changes they are causing in the environment. Thus, the abstract patterns of activity that represent the movements the organism is trying to achieve must constantly be referenced back to the initial sensory maps, not only for continuity but for determining how a given action is to be effectively carried out. Understanding speech must also require mappings back to the initial sensory maps, since a slight variation in a sound can alter the whole sense of a speaker's words. It is the initial mappings that are crucial to establishing the environmental context that we have seen is essential to establishing the sense and the significance of stimuli.

Epilogue and Conclusion

A spy sitting in a music hall might want to locate the woman he has just heard say, "Nine o'clock tomorrow," and he may also want to enjoy the singer's "Casta Diva." One set of brain maps will locate the person who said "nine o'clock," while another set of maps will permit him to hear the "Casta Diva" for his own pleasure. The sounds have been categorized in different ways by his brain in accordance with his adaptive needs: business and pleasure.

Later that evening the spy may realize he has forgotten the face of the woman he was shadowing during the concert. Annoyed, he hums the melody of "Casta Diva" and he is quite surprised to realize that in his imagination it is being sung by the woman he was following. This suggests that memory is not an exact repetition of an image in one's brain, but a recategorization. Recategorizations occur when the connections between the neuronal groups in different maps are temporarily strengthened. Recategorization of objects or events depends on motion as well as sensation, and it is a skill acquired in the course of experience. We recollect information in different contexts; this requires the activation of different maps interacting in ways that differ from those of our initial encounter with the information and that lead to its recategorization. We do not simply store images or bits but become more richly endowed with the *capacity to categorize* in connected ways.

Memory as recategorization is one of the deep implications of Edelman's theory of neuronal group selection. In a remarkable book published in 1932 and entitled *Remembering*, the English psychologist Frederic C. Bartlett sketched out the view to which Edelman's work has given a precision and a physiological justification:

Remembering is not the re-excitation of innumerable fixed, lifeless and fragmentary traces. It is an imaginative reconstruction, or construction, built out of the relation of our attitude towards a whole active mass of organized past reactions or experience, and to a little outstanding detail which commonly appears in image or in language form. It is thus hardly ever really exact, even in the most rudimentary cases of rote recapitulation, and it is not at all important that it should be so.[14]

It is this quality of memory that Freud, too, sought to capture. Believing that memories must leave permanent traces, and unable to see how a perceptual structure could remain open to new perceptions if it were altered by previous stimuli, he constructed a theory quite different from the view of brain function presented here.

Unable to accept that fragmentary memories may well be fragmentary, Freud assumed memories were fixed. In dispensing with fixed memories and replacing them with memory as categorization, Edelman's theory represents a radical departure from previous thought, and may well open the way for a broader and deeper view of human psychology.

Each person, according to his theory, is unique: his or her perceptions are to some degree creations, and his or her memories are part of an ongoing process of imagination. A mental life cannot be reduced to molecules. Human intelligence is not just knowing more, but reworking, recategorizing, and thus generalizing information in new and surprising ways. It could be that inappropriate categorizations from damaged maps cause psychoses, just as the inability to correlate the succession of objects or events in time may be largely responsible for the loss of specific memories in some cases of amnesia.

In its present form, Edelman's theory is concerned with the formation of perceptual categories. The question of higher mental functions—ultimately, language and consciousness—is not considered, though, as Edelman has claimed, the theory could be extended to encompass them. The formation of perceptual categories, his theory claims, cannot be reduced to a few simple physiological mechanisms, or rules. Rather, the complexity and variability of the procedures needed for categorization are suggested by the multiple abstract mappings based on the selectional principles described in the theory. The simulations, such as Darwin II, that Edelman and his colleagues have developed demonstrate that these selectional principles can form the basis of perceptual categorization. It remains to be shown how explicitly these simulations correspond to the workings of the brain.

If, however, it is possible to form categories with a relatively limited number of rules or, in a broader sense, if various mental functions could be performed by the brain in accordance with a few simple rules, then we would have good reason to question Edelman's theory. A reinterpretation of the clinical evidence, as argued in part I of this book, suggests, on the contrary, that higher mental function cannot be accounted for by relatively fixed procedures. Indeed, Edelman's theory confronts the very issues, categorization and generalization, that appear to be fundamental to any understanding of higher mental function. It gives us an intuitive sense, at the very least, of what the biological basis of mental life might be. The evolutionary principles at the heart of the theory are those on which the extraordinary advances of modern biology have been built.

Thus, while Edelman's theory is not directly concerned with higher mental function, it is not difficult to imagine how it might be expanded to help us understand the neurophysiological basis of language. Of course, language is acquired in society, but our ability to use it, to reconceive the world around us constantly, is, at least in part, a reflection of the multiple mappings and remappings that appear to be central to brain function.[15] Such a view reinforces the idea that no two brains can be, or ever will be, alike. Edelman's theory of neuronal group selection challenges those who claim that science views individual human beings and other animals as reproducible machines, and that science is little concerned with the unique attributes of individuals and the sources of that uniqueness. Humanism never had a better defense.

APPENDIX A

Word Blindness as
a Sensory Defect

In 1887 James Ross suggested that word blindness is a sensory—not a memory—defect. In his book *On Aphasia: Being a Contribution to the Subject of the Dissolution of Speech from Cerebral Disease* (London: J. & A. Churchill, 1887), he wrote:

There is . . . no difficulty in comprehending that complete blindness is a sensory paralysis; and it is also comparatively easy to realise that the profound amblyopia, in which the subject sees the form of an object without being able to appreciate its colour, is a partial sensory paralysis. Now, suppose that a person has his eyes directed to a piece of soap on the table, which is not in any way disguised so as to appear to the healthy eye other than it is, and yet he grasps it and puts it to his mouth as something to be eaten, would it not at once be suspected that that person was partially blind? This action might, of course, result from moral perversity, without any degree of blindness; but defective vision might lead to such an error of judgment as would give rise to it in the absence of any other mental peculiarity. In other words, a certain patch of colour falling upon a defective organ of vision failed to arouse in consciousness certain qualities belonging to the object, while it suggested other qualities which did not belong to it, and thus led to a serious error in judgment. When, therefore, the presentation of a common object to the eye fails to revive in consciousness certain previously well-known qualities belonging to the object, this may be taken as a sign of a partial paralysis of vision. When, for example, the general paralytic patient described by Fürstner failed to recognise that a coin placed in his hand was a money tender, he manifested partial blindness. His conduct, doubtless, also revealed loss of memory and defective judgment, but it did not differ in any essential respect from the conduct of a person who, from having lost the sense of colour owing to advancing white atrophy of the optic discs, mistakes a sovereign for a shilling. In the case of white atrophy, it is at once recognised that the mistaken conduct was the result of partial blindness; but when we pass from the non-revival of the more common properties of matter, such as is met with in cases of achromatopsia, to the non-revival of the less common properties, such as is met with in the disorders already named partial perceptive blindness and deafness, and in word-blindness and word-deafness, we only pass from a general to a special form of partial sensory paralysis. That word-deafness is a partial sensory paralysis may be aptly illustrated by my own mental condition with regard to the French language. I can read French, especially French medical literature, with nearly as much facility as English, but in listening to a conversation in French I am almost absolutely word-deaf. I can detect a few common verbs, pronouns, and adjectives, but hardly ever a noun, and, on the whole, the conversation is to me a series of sounds which blend with one another in inextricable confusion. Another peculiarity is that if I were asked to give the French name of any object presented to me, even including my bodily organs, I would fail, without considerable time for thought, in probably nine trials out of ten; but if the French name were pointed out to me on a printed page, I would instantly identify the object. I am also unable to write French to dictation, but can copy from a written or printed page, and with a full understanding of the meaning of what is written. My condition with regard to the French language is closely analogous to the condition of James

Appendix A

Lee . . . with regard to the English, and, indeed, all forms of language. He understands scarcely any word uttered in his hearing, and cannot name correctly any object presented to him; but when he sees the name in written or printed characters, he immediately identifies the object. He can also copy from a written or printed page, and understands the meaning of what he has written, but he is unable to write to dictation anything beyond his name and address. My disabilities with regard to the French language are manifestly due to the fact that my ear has not been educated, or in other words, to the fact that the necessary structure has not been organised in my auditory cortical centre; while the disabilities of Lee are due to the fact that the structure which had been organised in his auditory cortical centre is now destroyed by disease; in the one case there is a want of evolution of the necessary organisation, in the other there is a dissolution of a previously acquired structure. Similar remarks apply to word-blindness, although I am unable to illustrate the condition from my own experience so adequately as word-deafness. It appears to me, however, that the condition of Robert Marshall . . . , when looking at a printed page of English is, in some respects, similar to my own when looking at a page of Hebrew text. On scanning a page of Hebrew text, I not only cannot decipher a word, or even a letter, but I have even difficulty in imagining how any other person can attach a definite meaning to such a confused assemblage of dots and dashes. It is quite conceivable that I might have acquired the power of thinking and conversing in Hebrew without having learnt to read the language, and had I done so, my mental state would have been closely analogous to that of Marshall, with regard to English. I should then be able to name all objects presented to me, and to converse in Hebrew as Marshall does in English, and like him, I should be unable to read a printed page or to decipher a single letter. I should be able, like some of the subjects of word-blindness, to copy printed words in Hebrew in printed and written in written characters, and without being capable of attaching any meaning to what I had copied, though, unlike most of those who suffer from word-blindness, I should be unable to write to dictation. But notwithstanding the great similarity existing between cases in which there is a dissolution of one of the sensory mechanisms of speech and those in which the mechanism has been imperfectly evolved, yet the former present mental peculiarities which are not paralleled in the latter. For instance, if I were asked to write down the French phrase of "It is a fine day," I should never write anything so totally unlike it as "whiskey," as James Lee . . . did; and if I were asked to read from a printed page of Hebrew, I should not, even supposing I were able to converse in the language, give utterance, like Robert Marshall . . . to my own composition, fully believing that I was interpreting correctly the text before me. It need hardly be expected, however, that the brutal dissolution of nerve centres by sudden disease, like the softening caused by the occlusion of an artery, will ever exactly parallel in its results a simple arrest of the organisation of the same nerve centres at a particular stage of their evolution. On the whole, then, it may be concluded from physiological considerations, conjoined with the results obtained from post-mortem dissections, that word-blindness and word-deafness are a partial sensory paralysis, resulting from damage of the visual and auditory cortical centres respectively. [Pp. 107–9]

APPENDIX B

Memory "Flashbacks" Recorded by Penfield and Perot

The full transcripts of the recordings made during electrical stimulation of the brain, as published by Wilder Penfield and Phanor Perot in 1963 ("The Brain's Record of Auditory and Visual Experience," *Brain*, vol. 86), are as follows:*

*Numbers refer to area stimulated, as noted in accompanying diagrams. Text and figures reprinted courtesy of Oxford University Press.

Case 3: R. W., a twenty-three-year-old man (pp. 616–17)

At the time of stimulation the following experiential responses were produced

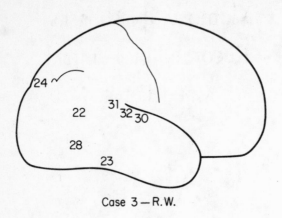

Case 3 — R.W.

22. He said nothing for a little interval, and then he said, "Oh, gee, gosh, robbers are coming at me with guns!" He heard nothing, he just saw them coming at him. The robbers seemed to have been coming at an angle from the left. When asked if they came in front of him, he said no they were behind him.

This seems to be the reproduction not of a real event, but of a fantasy or a dream drawn from the reading of a comic book, a silent fantasy devoid of auditory components.

23. "Pain in my forehead, and there was a robber. He wasn't in front, he was off to the left side."

24. "Yes, the robbers, they are coming after me."

Following this stimulation there was after-discharge.

. . .

28. "Oh gosh! There they are, my brother is there. He is aiming an air rifle at me." His eyes moved slowly to the left. The figures seemed to disappear before the cessation of the stimulus. When asked, he said his brother was walking toward him, and the gun was loaded. When asked where he was, he said at his house, in the yard. His other little brother was there, that was all. When asked if he felt scared when he saw his brother, he said, "Yes." When asked if he always felt scared when he saw the robbers, he said, "Yes."

30. "I heard someone speaking, my mother telling one of my aunts to come up tonight."

31. "Would you do it again, please?"

31. Repeated. After a pause, he said, "The same as before. My mother was telling my aunt over the telephone to come up and visit us tonight." When asked how he knew she was talking over the telephone, he said he did not see her, but from the way his aunt's voice sounded when she answered he knew it was over the telephone.

32. "My mother is telling my brother he has got his coat on backwards. I can just hear them." When asked if he remembered it, he said, "Oh yes, just before I came here." When asked if he thought these things were like dreams, he said, "No." When asked what it was like, he said, "It is just like I go into a daze."

Case 22: G. Le., a twenty-nine-year-old woman (p. 635)

The left temporal lobe was exposed at operation and these responses elicited.

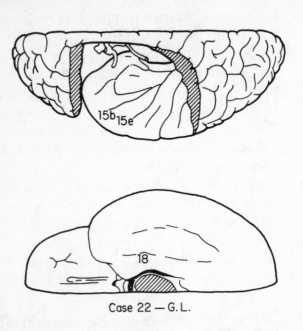

Case 22 — G. L.

15b. Stimulation at a depth of 2 cm. She reported, "Something coming to me from somewhere. A dream." When asked whether it was like an attack, she said, "Yes." [Note: *attack* refers to epileptic seizures. Patient had epilepsy.]

15b. Repeated, four minutes later, without warning. Dr. Roberts, who was sitting beneath the protective drapes with the patient, spoke to her and made gestures with his hand during the stimulation and she did not reply. After cessation of stimulation, she was silent for a time (there was a small electrographic seizure). When asked if she noticed what Dr. Roberts did, she replied, "I don't know what he did, I was trying to see what they were doing. The scenery seemed to be different from the one just before. I think there were people there, but I could not swear to it. That is what I call an attack." When asked again about the gestures Dr. Roberts had made, she said, "Yes, I saw his hand. I see the people in this world and in that world too, at the same time."

15e. Stimulation at a depth of 1½ cm. She said, "Wait a minute, something flashed over me, something I dreamt."

18. Stimulation just posterior to the uncus, after removal of the anterior part of the temporal lobe, in the vicinity of the cut uncus. She said, "I keep having dreams."

18. Repeated. "I keep seeing things—I keep dreaming of things."

Case 36: M. M., a twenty-six-year-old woman. This case includes the following hallucination recorded in the hospital during an attack of epilepsy. (Pp. 649–51)

"She had the same flash-back several times. These had to do with her cousin's house or the trip there—a trip she has not made for ten to fifteen years but used to make often as a child. She is in a motor car which had stopped before a railway crossing. The details are vivid. She can see the swinging light at the crossing. The train is going by—it is pulled by a locomotive passing from the left to right and she sees coal smoke coming out of the engine and flowing back over the train. On her right there is a big chemical plant and she remembers smelling the odor of the chemical plant.

The windows of the automobile seem to be down and she seems to be sitting on the right side and in the back. She sees the chemical plant as a big building with a half-fence next to the road. There is a large flat parking space. The plant is a big rambling building—no definite shape to it. There are many windows."

Whether this is actually true or not she does not know but it looks like that in the flashes. She thinks she hears the rumble of the train. It is made up of black flat-top cars full of cinders— the kind they use for work on the road. In another flash-back she says she sees her cousin's home and she is in it. She smells coffee—'They always have coffee,' and 'It is part of the atmosphere of the house.' "

The foregoing experiential hallucination is of particular interest because of the complex olfactory component. It is the only example we have recorded of a specific and identifiable olfactory experience in a seizure pattern. Gowers (1901)* mentioned a patient in whose attacks there invariably appeared before him an old woman in a brown-stuff dress, "who offered him something which had the smell of Tonquin beans," however, this may well have been a rather unspecific pleasant odor. . . .

*W. R. Gowers, *Epilepsy and Other Chronic Convulsive Diseases*, 2nd ed. (London, 1901).

Appendix B

The following experiential responses were produced with stimulation.

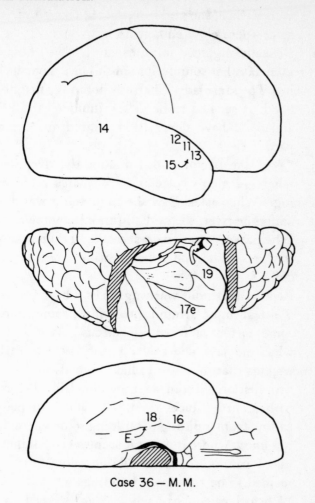

Case 36 — M. M.

11. She said, "I heard something familiar, I do not know what it was."

11. Repeated without warning. "Yes, sir, I think I heard a mother calling her little boy somewhere. It seemed to be something that happened years

ago." When asked if she knew who it was, she said, "Somebody in the neighborhood where I live." When asked, she said it seemed as though she was somewhere close enough to hear.

11. Repeated eighteen minutes later. "Yes, I hear the same familiar sounds, it seems to be a woman calling. The same lady. That was not in the neighborhood. It seemed to be at the lumber yard." She added, "I have never been around any lumber yard."

13. "Yes, I heard voices down along the river somewhere—a man's voice and a woman's voice, calling." When asked how she could tell it was down along the river, she said, "I think I saw the river." When asked what river, she said, "I do not know, it seems to be one I was visiting when I was a child."

13. Repeated without warning. "Yes, I hear voices, it is late at night, around the carnival somewhere—some sort of a travelling circus." When asked what she saw, she said, "I just saw lots of big wagons that they use to haul animals in."

12. Stimulation without warning. She said, "I seemed to hear little voices then. The voices of people calling from building to building somewhere. I do not know where it is but it seems very familiar to me. I cannot see the buildings now, but they seemed to be run-down buildings."

14. "I heard voices. My whole body seemed to be moving back and forth, particularly my head."

14. Repeated. "I heard voices."

17e. Stimulation at a depth of 1½ cm. toward the superior surface of the temporal lobe. The patient said, "Oh, I had the same very, very familiar memory in an office somewhere. I could see the desks. I was there and someone was calling to me, a man leaning on a desk with a pencil in his hand."

11. Repeated forty minutes after the last stimulation at this point. "I had a flash of familiar memory, but I do not know what it was."

13. Repeated three times thirty minutes after the last stimulation at this point. "Nothing."

15. Stimulation of the inferior aspect of the first temporal convolution. "I had one of those very familiar memories."

16. Stimulation in the general vicinity of the uncus or just lateral to it. The patient said, "I had a little memory—a scene in a play. They were talking and I could see it. It was just seeing it in my memory."

18. Stimulation more posteriorly on the undersurface of the temporal lobe. "A very familiar memory of a girl talking to me."

19. Stimulation of the superior surface of the first temporal convolution adjacent to the uncus. "I feel very close to an attack—I think I am going to have one—a familiar memory."

E. Stimulation without warning. She said, "Oh, it hurts, and that feeling of familiarity—a familiar memory—the place where I hang my coat up, where I go to work."

APPENDIX C

An Associative
Recall Experiment
on Darwin II

In one experiment, for example, an X was presented on the input array (see figure C.1). The Darwin network responded with a typical topological response in the second panel, and with an abstraction of that response (which was not topological) in the third panel. The Wallace network, on the other hand, abstracted its trace, or tactile, response to a group in the third panel which, through reentrant connections that happened to run between the two groups, resulted in a strengthening of those connections. Subsequently a plus sign was presented on the input array, causing the same group response in the third panel of the Wallace network as the X had caused. However, the response in the third panel of the Darwin network, since it is concerned not with general features but with the unique attributes of a stimulus, is not the same as the one for the X. Therefore reentrant connections are established between this new

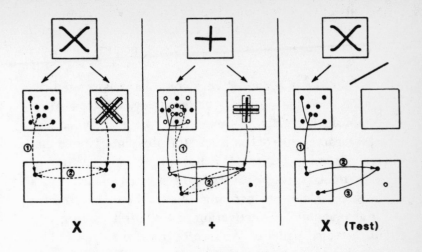

Figure C.1.

Schematic views of Darwin II showing three stages in an associative recall experiment. Filled circles represent active groups; open circles, inactive groups. Solid lines between groups represent connections selectively strengthened; dashed lines represent connections activated for the first time. Numerals enclosed in circles label pathways that are activated at successive times.

SOURCE: Figure and caption from George N. Reeke, Jr., and Gerald N. Edelman, "Selective Networks and Recognition Automata," *Annals of the New York Academy of Sciences* 426 (1984): 195.

group in the Darwin network and the old group in the Wallace network which responded to both the X and the plus sign. Now when the Darwin II is presented with an X on the input array, so that only the Darwin side of the network is activated (the visual system, but not the tactile system, is active), the abstract group, or a similar group of the X, is activated in the third panel of Darwin. Then the reentry connections activate the X/plus-sign group in the Wallace third panel. And reentry again activates the plus-sign group in the third panel of Darwin. The X and the plus-sign stimuli have been associated by the network. If novel stimuli related to an X or a plus sign are presented to the system, these stimuli will be generalized, just as the X and the plus sign were associated.

While the Wallace network could have associated the X and the plus sign in a general way, the association established with the Darwin network included the unique attributes of the X and the plus sign. Notice that recognition in Darwin II is not simply the activation of a particular group but rather a pattern of activity, a cross-correlation of mappings. Nor is there a simple idea of association. The activation of the X/plus-sign group in the third panel of Wallace by itself does not tell us whether an X or a plus sign is present on the input array. In figure C.1, in one case, its activation indicates the presence of an X and, in the other, a plus sign. It does, of course, tell us that the general class of X/plus sign is present on the input array. Even the apparently unique response of the plus-sign group in panel 3 of Darwin does not, for sure, indicate the presence of a plus sign. This can be learned only from the entire pattern of activity of the panel and its interactions with the other panels.

NOTES

PART 1 Against Localization

1. Paul Broca, "Perte de la parole, ramollissement chronique et destruction partielle du lobe antérieur gauche du cerveau," *Bulletin de la Société d'Anthropologie* 2 (18 April 1861): 235–37. (Also in H. Hécaen and J. Dubois, *La Naissance de la Neuropsychologie du Langage: 1825–1865* [Paris: Flammarion, 1969], p. 61.) (Translations from Hécaen and Dubois by the author.)

2. Paul Broca, "Remarques sur le siège de la faculté du langage articulé, suivies d'une observation d'aphémie (perte de la parole)," *Bulletin de la Société d'Anthropologie,* 2nd series, vol. 6 (August 1861): 330–57. (See, too, Hécaen and Dubois, *La Naissance,* pp. 61–91, esp. p. 75.)

3. Broca, "Remarques sur le siège." In Hécaen and Dubois, *La Naissance,* pp. 77–78.

4. In Hécaen and Dubois, *La Naissance,* pp. 64–65.

5. Ibid., p. 65.

6. Ibid.

7. Ludwig Lichtheim, "On Aphasia," *Brain* 7 (January 1885): 433–84. Quotes on pp. 435–36 and 436–37.

8. Carl Wernicke, "The Symptom Complex of Aphasia," in *Boston Studies in the Philosophy of Science,* vol. 4, ed. and trans. R. S. Cohen and M. W. Watofsky (Boston: O. Reidel, 1966), p. 36.

9. Cited by Jules Baillarger in Hécaen and Dubois, *La Naissance,* p. 182.

10. Adolf Kussmaul, *Die Störungen der Sprache. Versuch einer Pathologie der Sprache* (Leipzig, 1881), p. 177. (Translation in Frederic Bateman, *On Aphasia, or Loss of Speech, and The Localisation of the Faculty of Articulate Language* [London: J. & A. Churchill, 1890], p. 223.)

11. C. Giraudeau, "Note sur un cas de Surdité Psychique," *Revue de Médecine* 2 (1882): 446. (Translation in Bateman, *On Aphasia,* pp. 220–22.)

12. Bateman, *On Aphasia,* pp. 224, 222.

13. Ibid., p. 221.

14. Jules Dejerine, "Sur un cas de cécité verbale avec agraphie, suivi

d'autopsie," *Comptes Rendus Hebdomadaires des Séances et Mémoires de la Société de Biologie,* 9th series, vol. 3 (the meeting of 21 March 1891), p. 197. (Translation by the author.)

15. Ibid., p. 200.

16. Ibid., p. 198.

17. Jules Dejerine, "Contribution à l'étude anatomo-pathologique et clinique des différentes variétés de cécité verbale," *Comptes Rendus Hebdomadaires des Séances et Mémoires de la Société de Biologie,* 9th series, vol. 4 (the meeting of 27 February 1892), pp. 64–65. (Translation by the author.)

18. Ibid., pp. 65–66.

19. Ibid., pp. 74–78.

20. Ibid., pp. 88–89.

21. Richard Mayeux and Eric R. Kandel, "Natural Language, Disorders of Language, and Other Localizable Disorders of Cognitive Functioning," in *Principles of Neural Science,* 2nd ed., ed. E. R. Kandel and J. H. Schwartz (New York: Elsevier, 1985), pp. 696–97.

22. Dejerine, "Contribution à l'étude," p. 89.

23. Ibid., p. 87.

24. Jules Dejerine, *Sémiologie des Affections du Système Nerveux* (Paris: Masson et Cie, 1926), p. 95.

25. Dejerine, "Contribution à l'étude," pp. 71–72.

26. In Kandel and Schwartz, *Principles of Neural Science,* p. 697.

27. Normal Geschwind, "Disconnexion Syndromes in Animals and Man," in *Selected Papers on Language and the Brain* (Dordrecht, Holland: Reidel, 1974), p. 149.

28. Ibid., p. 148.

29. Jean-Baptiste Charcot, "Sur un appareil destiné à évoquer les images motrices graphiques chez les sujets atteints de cecité verbale," *Comptes Rendus Hebdomadaires des Séances et Mémoires de la Société de Biologie,* 9th series, vol. 4 (the meeting of 11 June 1892), pp. 239–40.

30. Ibid., p. 240.

31. Dejerine, "Contribution à l'étude," p. 87.

32. Dejerine, *Sémiologie des Affections,* pp. 148–49.

33. Nikolai Aleksandrovich Bernstein, "The Coordination and Regulation of Movements," in *Human Motor Actions: Bernstein Reassessed,* ed. H. T. A. Whiting (Amsterdam: Elsevier Science Publishers, 1984), p. 105.

34. Ibid., pp. 94, 95.

35. John Hughlings-Jackson, "On Affections of Speech from Disease of the Brain," *Brain* 2 (April 1879–January 1880): 327n, 328.

Notes

36. Ibid., pp. 218–19.

37. Ibid., p. 222.

38. Ibid., p. 220n.

39. Bateman, *On Aphasia*, pp. 201–202. (Author's revision of Bateman's translation.)

40. Armand Trousseau, *Clinique Médicale de l'Hôtel-Dieu de Paris* (Paris: Baillière et fils, 1877). In Hécaen and Dubois, *La Naissance*, p. 200.

41. Hughlings-Jackson, "On Affections of Speech," p. 203.

42. Sigmund Freud, "Inhibitions, Symptoms and Anxiety," in *The Standard Edition of the Complete Psychological Works of Sigmund Freud*, vol. 20 (London: The Hogarth Press and The Institute of Psychoanalysis, 1959), p. 120.

43. Sigmund Freud, "Notes upon a Case of Obsessional Neurosis," in *The Standard Edition*, vol. 10 (1955), p. 196.

44. Sigmund Freud, "From the History of an Infantile Neurosis," in *The Standard Edition*, vol. 17 (1955), p. 49.

45. Sigmund Freud, "An Outline of Psycho-analysis," in *The Standard Edition*, vol. 23 (1964), pp. 167–68.

46. Sigmund Freud, "The Unconscious," in *The Standard Edition*, vol. 14 (1957), p. 186.

47. Ibid., pp. 166–67.

48. Sigmund Freud, *On Aphasia* (New York: International Universities Press, 1953), p. 103.

49. Ibid., p. 57.

50. Sigmund Freud, "Notes upon a Case of Obsessional Neurosis," p. 243.

51. Quotations from Marcel Proust, *Remembrance of Things Past*, from the translation by Andreas Mayor. Vol. 2, *The Past Recaptured*, copyright © 1970 by Random House, pp. 999, 1001, 1078. Reprinted by permission.

52. Quotations in the original French from Marcel Proust, *A la Recherche du Temps Perdu*, vol. 3 (Paris: Bibliothèque de la Pléiade, © Editions Gallimard, 1954), pp. 869, 871, 970.

53. A. A. Low, "A Case of Agrammatism in the English Language," *Archives of Neurology and Psychiatry* 25 (1931): 558, 561.

54. Ibid., p. 564.

55. Ibid., pp. 566, 567.

56. Ibid., p. 577.

57. Aleksandr Romanovich Luria, *The Mind of a Mnemonist* (Middlesex, England: Penguin Books, 1975), p. 33.

58. John C. Marshall, "Routes and Representations in the Processing of Written Language," *Motor and Sensory Processes of Language,* ed. Eric Keller and Myrna Gopnik (Hillsdale, N.J.: Erlbaum, 1987), p. 242. See, too, John C. Marshall and Freda Newcombe, "Patterns of Paralexia: A Psycholinguistic Approach," *Journal of Psycholinguistic Research* 2, no. 3 (1973): 175–99.

59. Marshall and Newcombe, "Patterns of Paralexia," pp. 183–84.

60. John C. Marshall and Freda Newcombe, "Syntactic and Semantic Errors in Paralexia," *Neuropsychologia* 4 (1966): 169–76. Quote is on page 175. See also J. J. Katz and J. Fodor, in *Language* 39 (1963): 170–210.

61. Elizabeth Warrington, "The Selective Impairment of Semantic Memory," *Quarterly Journal of Experimental Psychology* 27 (1975): 646.

62. Elizabeth K. Warrington and T. Shallice, "Category Specific Semantic Impairments," *Brain* 107 (1984): 838.

63. Elizabeth K. Warrington, "Neuropsychological Studies of Verbal Semantic Systems," *Philosophical Transactions of the Royal Society of London* B 295 (1981): 421.

64. Ibid., p. 422.

PART 2 Language as Gesture and the Recognition of Speech

1. Michael Studdert-Kennedy, "The Phoneme as a Perceptuomotor Structure," in *Language Perception and Production,* ed. A. Allport, D. McKay, W. Prinz, and E. Scheerer (New York: Academic Press, 1987), p. 76

2. Ibid. See, too, Charles A. Ferguson and Carol B. Farwell, "Words and Sounds in Early Language Acquisition," *Language* 51 (1975): 419–39.

3. Breyne Arlene Moskowitz, "The Acquisition of Language," *Scientific American* (November 1978): 106.

4. Studdert-Kennedy, "Phoneme as Perceptuomotor Structure," p. 78.

5. For a superb recent discussion of Liberman's work, see Alvin M. Liberman and Ignatius G. Mattingly, "The Motor Theory of Speech Perception Revised," *Cognition* 21 (1985): 1–36.

6. Nikolai Aleksandrovich Bernstein, "The Coordination and Regulation of Movements," in *Human Motor Actions: Bernstein Reassessed,* ed. H. T. A. Whiting (Amsterdam: Elsevier Science Publishers, North-Holland Publishing Company, 1984), p. 116.

Notes

PART 3   Machine Recognition

1. David Marr, *Vision* (San Francisco: W. H. Freeman, 1982), p. 102.

2. Thomas Hobbes, *Leviathan*, ed. C. B. Macpherson (Middlesex, England: Penguin Books, 1968), p. 186.

3. Marr, *Vision*, p. 356.

4. Philip J. Kellman and Elizabeth S. Spelke, "Perception of Partly Occluded Objects in Infancy," *Cognitive Psychology* 15 (1983): 522.

5. David E. Rumelhart, James L. McClelland, and the PDP Research Group, *Parallel Distributed Processing: Explorations in the Microstructure of Cognition*, vol. 1 (Cambridge, Mass.: MIT Press, 1986), p. 12.

6. Ibid., vol. 2, p. 241.

7. Margaret Donaldson, "Language: Learning Word Meanings," in *The Oxford Companion to the Mind*, ed. Richard L. Gregory (New York: Oxford University Press, 1987), pp. 421–23.

8. W. V. Quine, "Symbols," in ibid., pp. 763–65.

9. Arthur R. V. Cooper, "Chinese Evidence on the Evolution of Language," in ibid., pp. 142–46.

10. Noam Chomsky, "Language: Chomsky's Theory," in ibid., pp. 419–21.

PART 4   Neural Darwinism: A New Approach to Memory and Perception

1. Sigmund Freud, *The Interpretation of Dreams*, in *The Standard Edition of the Complete Psychological Works of Sigmund Freud*, vol. 5 (London: The Hogarth Press and The Institute of Psycho-analysis, 1959), p. 538.

2. Freud, *The Standard Edition*, vol. 1, "Letter 52," pp. 233, 235.

3. A. R. Damasio, P. J. Eslinger, H. Damasio, G. W. Van Hoesen, and S. Cornell, "Multi-Modal Amnesic Syndrome Following Bilateral Temporal and Basal Forebrain Damage," *Archives of Neurology* 42 (March 1985): 252–59.

4. See Brenda Milner's discussion of H. M.'s memory loss, "Amnesia Following Operation on the Temporal Lobes," in *Amnesia*, ed. C. W. M. Whitty and O. L. Zanguil (London: Butterworth's, 1966), pp. 109–33.

5. Horace M. Abel and W. S. Colman, quoted in Bernard Hollander, *The Mental Symptoms of Brain Disease* (London: Rebman Limited, 1910), pp. 40–41, 43.

6. Ibid., p. 42.

7. Wilder Penfield, "Consciousness, Memory and Man's Conditioned Reflexes," in *On the Biology of Learning*, ed. K. Pribram (New York: Harcourt, Brace & World, 1969), p. 152.

8. Wilder Penfield and Phanor Perot, "The Brain's Record of Auditory and Visual Experience," *Brain* 86, pt. 4 (1963): 617, 635, 650. (See appendix B for full record of each case.)

9. Pierre Gloor, André Olivier, Luis F. Quesney, Frederick Andermann, and Sandra Horowitz, "The Role of the Limbic System in Experimental Phenomena of Temporal Lobe Epilepsy," *Annals of Neurology* 12 (1982): 140.

10. Ibid., p. 142.

11. Elizabeth F. Loftus and Geoffrey R. Loftus, "On the Permanence of Stored Information in the Human Brain," *American Psychologist* 35 (1980): 413, 414. Quotes from Penfield and Perot from "The Brain's Record of Auditory and Visual Experience," p. 692. Quote from Mahl et al. from George F. Mahl, Albert Rothenberg, Jose M. R. Delgado, and Hannibal Hamlin, *Psychosomatic Medicine* 26 (1964): 358.

See, too, Gloor's interesting remarks, again suggesting a failure to establish any contextual setting, though he does not note this point:

He [Penfield] assumed that the vivid details which often characterize such experimental responses are evidence that all the details of a previous experience are recorded in the brain and can be "replayed" in their original sequence when epileptic discharge or electrical stimulation reactivates certain circuits in the temporal cortex. However, hallucinations of scenes never experienced before, yet at times nevertheless related to some remembered event may also be evoked by such stimulations or epileptic discharge and can be as vivid and detailed as those of a true memory flashback. It therefore seems unlikely that electrical stimulation or seizure discharges involving temporolimbic circuits replay a faithful record of past events. The fragmentary character of these experimental phenomena also argue against such an interpretation. Perhaps it is rather that temporal epileptic discharge or electrical stimulation, by a process as yet unknown, activates neuronal networks that vividly bring forth the elementary and ultimately affective impact of a given experience, its existential context and immediacy in the Proustian sense, as opposed to a detailed record of an unfolding story or the recollection of some self-directed action or mental effort which Penfield and Perot found unaccountably missing among their observations. Such experimental "flashbacks" occur at times in the course of ordinary living in normal persons. Odor stimuli are particularly apt to activate vivid feelings of

Notes

finding oneself in an almost forgotten place from one's remote past, providing a further indication that limbic circuits are involved in their evocation. [Gloor et al., "The Role of the Limbic System," p. 142]

12. For more details on Edelman's work, as discussed in the rest of part 4, see: "Through a Computer Darkly: Group Selection and Higher Brain Function," *Bulletin of the American Academy of Arts and Sciences* 36, no. 1 (October 1982): 20–48; "Neural Darwinism: Population Thinking and Higher Brain Function," in *How We Know*, ed. Michael Shafto (Harper and Row, 1986), pp. 1–30; "Group Selection and Phasic Reentrant Signaling: A Theory of Higher Brain Function," in *The Mindful Brain*, ed. G. M. Edelman and V. B. Mountcastle (MIT Press, 1978), pp. 51–100; "Group Selection as the Basis for Higher Brain Function," in *The Organization of the Cerebral Cortex*, ed. F. O. Schmitt et al. (MIT Press, 1981), pp. 535–63; "Neuronal Group Selection in the Cerebral Cortex" (with Leif H. Finkel), in *Dynamic Aspects of Neocortical Function*, ed. G. M. Edelman, W. E. Gall, and W. M. Cowan (Wiley, 1984), pp. 653–95; "Cell Adhesion Molecules," *Science* 219 (4 February 1983): 450–57; "Expression of Cell Adhesion Molecules During Embryogenesis and Regeneration," *Experimental Cell Research* 161 (1984): 1–16; "Interaction of Synaptic Modification Rules Within Populations of Neurons" (with Leif H. Finkel), *Proceedings of the National Academy of Science* 82 (February 1985): 1291–95; "Selective Networks and Recognition Automata" (with George N. Reeke, Jr.), *Annals of the New York Academy of Sciences* 426 (1984): 181–201. By far the most interesting and complete discussion of Edelman's theory is to be found in his difficult but superb book *Neural Darwinism: The Theory of Neuronal Group Selection* (New York: Basic Books, 1987).

13. W. J. Gallin, C.-M. Chuong, L. H. Finkel, and G. M. Edelman, "Antibodies to Liver Cell Adhesion Molecule Perturb Inductive Interactions and Alter Feather Pattern and Structure," *Proceedings of the National Academy of Science U.S.A.*, vol. 83, pp. 8235–39.

14. Frederic C. Bartlett, *Remembering: A Study in Experimental and Social Psychology* (Cambridge: Cambridge University Press, 1964), p. 213.

15. The pattern of language acquisition discussed by Donaldson, in which children first learn the meaning of sentences and only later individual words, suggests that the brain may first be generalizing about the larger phonetic contours of the sentence, then about the phonetic boundaries that establish the individual words, and then about how the words are (grammatically) related to one another. One could imagine how a series of maps might abstract the larger phonetic contours of sentences, and how subsequently similar abstracting procedures might establish word boundaries with other maps ab-

stracting correlations among the words. In this view, language would be specific to human beings because it would depend on their having brains large enough, and with enough maps, to carry out these abstracting procedures, as well as a voice box for producing the necessary combinations of sounds.

In "Mind and Evolution," a manuscript I wrote in 1976–77, I described the relation of language to consciousness in the following terms:

Through language, through images of various kinds, man has created larger, more encompassing transformations of stimuli. The very nature of thought is a continual integration and transformation of givens and of the products of mind itself. The fact that every sentence we utter becomes in turn a new stimulus means that its meaning becomes transformed.

Understanding is the fitting of new images into old molds, transforming the old mold and the new image into a new entity. Perhaps, more than repetition, it is the capacity for transformation that is so fundamental to mental activity. A radical transformation has been imposed on visual, auditory and tactile images and this transformation has brought with it *human* consciousness. [Pp. 144–45, 151–52.]

Also, on p. 144 is the following passage which contains one of the main themes of the present book: "The nervous system can only approximate what it has already produced. We try to discipline it to be more sure of our reactions—but then there is always the unknown that suddenly alters the framework. Do these apparently fixed images always have the same meaning? Their context will vary with time and consequently their sense as well. In fact, one suspects that what appears to be a fixed image is an *approximate* reproduction of an earlier image."

INDEX

Agraphia, 37, 46; associated with inability to read, 30–31, 47; and argument for an independent writing center, 30

Ambiguous letter, deciphering with a PDP machine, 151, 152 (fig. 3.9)

Associations, cross-modal, 56

Auditory "illusion," 100

Auditory word representations, 5, 21, 22; destruction of, in word deafness, 25, 28

Axes of symmetry, 138–41; principal and secondary, 118 (fig. 3.1); use of, in deriving shape, 141

Baillarger, Jules, 70, 70–71*n*

Bartlett, Frederic C., 196–97

Bastian, Henry Charlton, 25

Bateman, Frederic, 28

Bell, Alexander Graham, 99

Bernstein, Nikolai Aleksandrovich, 59–61, 111–12, 153 (fig. 3.10); on localization of function and the problem of movement, 60–61, 153 (fig. 3.10); on Helmholtz's theory of sound perception, 111–12; on speech perception vs. the perception of music, 111–12

Biological variation, nature of, 171

Bouquinet, Marie, 26–31, 71; case study of, 26–27; Frederic Bateman on, 28; critique of Bateman's view on, 28–30

Brain function: computational approaches to (modularity), 122–36 (*see also* Context); development and, 181; Edelman's view of, 175 (*see also* Cell-adhesion molecules); and localization vs. holism, 4–5, 10–11, 12–16 (*see also individual authors*: Bastian, Dejerine, Exner, Flourens, Freud, Gall, Goltz, Hughlings-Jackson, Lichtheim, Penfield, Wernicke); maps and, 174, 183–89; and sorting information, 63–66 (*see also* Darwin II); Sperry's view of, 174–75; symbols and, 128*n*, 128–29, 136

Broca, Paul, 4, 13; and case of Tan, 16–18; and cursing, 16, 17, 69; and memory as procedure (motor memory), 18–21

Broca's aphasia, 24

Broca's area, 21

Burnet, MacFarlane, 173

Categorization: as basis of perception and recognition, 8, 162–63; and creation of categories, 193 (*see also* Maps); as creating sense of continuity (and Freudian notion of uncon-

225

Index

Index

229

Index

Index